Practice

Maths and English

BUMPER BOOK

Age 7–9
Years 3–4
Key Stage 2

Acknowledgements
p.14 Pamela Mordecai: 'Caribbean Counting Rhyme' from Spotlight on Poetry: Poems Around the World 1, collected by Brian Moses and David Orme (Collins Educational, 1999), reproduced by permission of HarperCollins Publishers Ltd.; **pp.16, 18** Jeff Kinney: Text, illustration and back cover from Diary of a Wimpy Kid: The Last Straw (Puffin Books, 2009), reproduced by permission of Penguin Books Ltd.; **p.20** Brenda Stones & Kay Hiatt: Playscript from Collins Primary Literacy – Pupil Book 1C (Collins Educational, n/e, 2008), reproduced by permission of HarperCollins Publishers Ltd.

Every effort has been made to trace all copyright holders, but if any have been inadvertently overlooked the Publishers will be pleased to make the necessary arrangements at the first opportunity.

Although every effort has been made to ensure that website addresses are correct at time of going to press, Hodder Education cannot be held responsible for the content of any website mentioned in this book. It is sometimes possible to find a relocated web page by typing in the address of the home page for a website in the URL window of your browser.

Hachette UK's policy is to use papers that are natural, renewable and recyclable products and made from wood grown in sustainable forests. The logging and manufacturing processes are expected to conform to the environmental regulations of the country of origin.

Orders: please contact Bookpoint Ltd, 130 Milton Park, Abingdon, Oxon OX14 4SB. Telephone: (44) 01235 827720. Fax: (44) 01235 400454. Lines are open 9.00a.m.–5.00p.m., Monday to Saturday, with a 24-hour message answering service. Visit our website at www.hoddereducation.co.uk.

© Brenda Stones, Steve Mills and Hilary Koll, Richard Cooper 2013
Teacher's tips © Najoud Ensaff and Matt Koster 2013
First published in 2013 exclusively for WHSmith by
Hodder Education
An Hachette UK Company
Carmelite House
50 Victoria Embankment
London EC4Y 0DZ

Impression number   10 9 8 7 6 5 4
Year   2018 2017 2016 2015

This edition has been updated, 2014, to reflect National Curriculum changes.

Cover illustration by Oxford Designers and Illustrators Ltd
Character illustrations: Beehive Illustration
All other illustrations Fakenham Prepress Solutions, Fakenham, Norfolk NR21 8NN
Typeset in Folio by Fakenham Prepress Solutions, Fakenham, Norfolk NR21 8NN
Printed in Spain

A catalogue record for this title is available from the British Library.

ISBN: 978 1444 188 677

Advice for parents

Maths and English Practice bumper book

The books in the *Practice* series are designed to practise and consolidate children's work in school. They are intended for children to complete on their own, but you may like to work with them for the first few pages.

This bumper book provides a selection of titles from the *Practice* range for children aged 7–9. This selection consists of two English titles: *English Practice* and *Writing and Punctuation Practice*; and two Maths titles: *Maths Practice* and *Problem Solving Practice*.

Details for all of the titles in the *Practice* Key Stage 2 series can be found on the inside front cover of this book.

When using this book with your child, the following points will help:

- Don't ask your child to do too much at once. A 'little and often' approach is a good way to start.
- Reward your child with lots of praise and encouragement. These should be enjoyable activities for them.
- Discuss with your child what they have learned and what they can do.
- The '**Get ready**' section provides a gentle warm-up for the topic covered on the page.
- The '**Let's practise**' section is usually the main activity. This section helps to consolidate understanding of the topic.
- The '**Have a go**' section is often a challenge or something interesting that your child can go away and do which is related to the topic. It may require your child to use everyday objects around the home.
- The '**How have I done?**' section at the end of the book is a short informal test that should be attempted when all the units have been completed. It is useful for spotting gaps in knowledge, which can then be revisited at a suitable moment.
- The '**Teacher's tips**' are written by practising classroom teachers. They give useful advice on specific topics or skills, to deepen your child's understanding and confidence and to help you help your child.

Contents

WRITING AND PUNCTUATION

MATHS

PROBLEM SOLVING

Welcome to Kids Club!

Hi, readers. My name's Charlie and I run Kids Club with my friend Abbie. Kids Club is an after-school club which is very similar to one somewhere near you.

We'd love you to come and join our club and see what we get up to!

I'm Abbie. Let's meet the kids who will work with you on the activities in this book.

My name's Jamelia. I look forward to Kids Club every day. The sports and games are my favourites, especially on Kids Camp in the school holidays.

Hi, I'm Megan. I've made friends with all the kids at Kids Club. I like the outings and trips we go on the best.

Hello, my name's Kim. Kids Club is a great place to chill out after school. My best friend is Alfie – he's a bit naughty but he means well!

I'm Amina. I like to do my homework at Kids Club. Charlie and Abbie are always very helpful. We're like one big happy family.

Greetings, readers, my name's Alfie! Everybody knows me here. Come and join our club; we'll have a wicked time together!

Now you've met us all, tell us something about yourself.
All the kids filled in a '**Personal Profile**' when they joined. Here's one for you to complete.

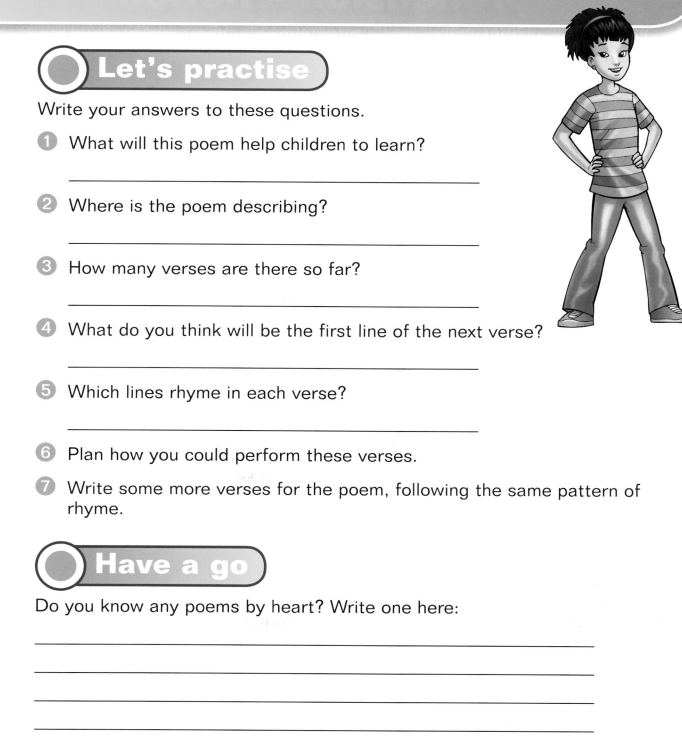

Let's practise

Write your answers to these questions.

1 What will this poem help children to learn?

_____

2 Where is the poem describing?

_____

3 How many verses are there so far?

_____

4 What do you think will be the first line of the next verse?

_____

5 Which lines rhyme in each verse?

_____

6 Plan how you could perform these verses.

7 Write some more verses for the poem, following the same pattern of rhyme.

Have a go

Do you know any poems by heart? Write one here:

_____

_____

_____

_____

_____

Teacher's tips

As you read the poem listen to the words at the end of each line. If any of these have the same endings, these are the words that rhyme! Remember, a verse is like a paragraph in a poem.

These two pages are about reading and understanding stories.

 **Get ready**

When we read a story, we need to understand not just what is happening, but also:

- what kind of story it is, e.g. fairy story, science fiction or humour
- who wrote it
- who the characters are, and what their characteristics are
- what the setting of the story is
- what might happen next.

Read this page from one of the Diary of a Wimpy Kid books, *The Last Straw*:

Monday
When me and Rowley got to our bus stop today, we found a nasty surprise. There was a piece of paper taped to our street sign, and it said that, effective today, our bus route was "rezoned". And what that means is now we have to WALK to school.

Well, I'd like to talk to the genius who came up with THAT idea, because our street is almost a quarter of a mile from the school.

Me and Rowley had to run to make it to school on time today. And what REALLY stunk was when our regular bus passed us by and it was full of kids from Whirley Street, the neighbourhood right next to ours.

13

Teacher's tips

For question 6, standard English is grammatically correct English – what you would write, not what you might say to someone. Decide whether it's grammatically correct to write *Me and Rowley went…* or *Rowley and I went…*?

Let's practise

Write your answers to these questions.

1 Why do you think the text is in handwriting?

_____

2 Why are some words in capitals?

_____

3 What does the heading tell you about the genre?

_____

4 What does the illustration add to the story?

_____

5 What country do they live in? How can you tell?

_____

6 Is 'me and Rowley' standard or non-standard English?

_____

7 What verb does 'stunk' come from? _____

8 What do you think will happen next? _____

_____

Have a go

What stories have you enjoyed reading?
Make a list here of some of your favourite
fiction:

These two pages are about understanding informational text.

When you are reading non-fiction or information, there are different things to look out for:

- the purpose of the information
- the layout of the page
- the use of illustrations to give information
- the different kinds of language used.

This is the back cover of the fiction book you started reading on page 16.

The back cover text is called the 'blurb'.

Read this blurb, and think about why it has been written.

Teacher's tips

Read the whole back cover twice. Then look at each question on page 19 in turn and look back at what you have read to find your answer.

Let's practise

Write your answers to these questions.

1 Where would you find a piece of text like this?

_____

2 What is the purpose of the text?

_____

3 Where does the first paragraph of text come from?

_____

4 Who has written the second paragraph of text?

_____

5 Why has the cartoon drawing been put there?

_____

6 Why is the single word from a newspaper put there?

_____

7 Why are there three other book covers shown?

_____

_____

8 What are the two websites mentioned?

_____

_____

Have a go

Now write the back cover blurb for a book you have really enjoyed.

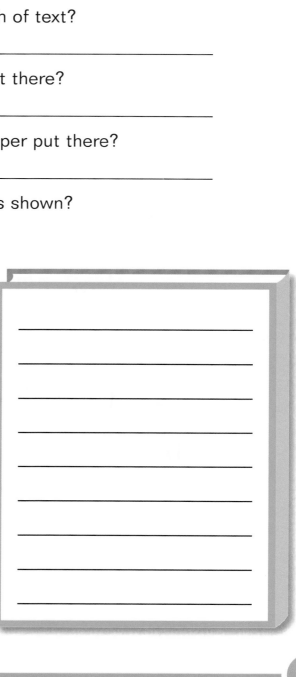

These two pages are about understanding what playscripts are for.

Get ready

A playscript is the text for reading a play.
It looks different from other kinds of text:

- the character's name is written before the lines they speak
- you have to think what expression to give that character's words
- there may be a 'narrator' who tells the audience what is happening
- there may also be instructions for performance, called 'stage directions'.

Read this short piece of playscript:

Narrator:	One day the farmer went to his field to pull up his biggest turnip. He could not pull up the turnip, so the farmer called his wife to help.
Farmer:	Wife! Wife! Help me pull up this turnip!
Narrator:	They still could not pull up the turnip, so the wife called her children to help.

Let's practise

Now build more words, using these prefixes.

Match each of these words to a prefix to make a new word, and write what the new word means.

**city   obey   read   climax   divide
market   decorate   graph**

Prefix	Meaning	New word	Meaning
dis-	not		
mis-	not		
re-	again		
sub-	under		
inter-	between		
super-	above		
anti-	against		
auto-	self		

Have a go

Write a sentence using two or more of these words with prefixes.

_____

_____

Teacher's tips

Remember, a dictionary can help you determine whether your new word exists. Look up the word in either a book or Internet dictionary to check whether it is a real word and to find out its meaning!

8: Spelling – suffixes

We can build new words by adding to the end of a word; this is called adding a **suffix**.

 **Get ready**

How do you spell words that end with the sound 'shun'? There are five possible answers!

Usually, the best clue is to go back to the spelling of the root word.

Spelling	When	Examples
-tion	The most common spelling. Use when the root word ends in **-t** or **-te**.	action
-sion	Use when the root word ends in **-d**.	expansion, extension
-ssion	Use when the root word ends in **-ss** or **-mit**.	expression, permission
-cian	Use when the root word ends in **-c** or **-cs**. These are usually people's jobs.	musician, magician
-shion	These are just exceptions! They tend to come from foreign words.	cushion, fashion

Can you add more words to the grid? Check them in your dictionary, to get the right spelling.

Let's practise

Here are some words that can all have a suffix
sounding like 'shun'.

Fill in the right spellings!

complete	completion
transit	
omit	
electric	
inflate	
confess	
admit	
politics	
c ect	
fect	
it	
ssess	

Have a go

e sound is more like 'zhun', the spelling wil be **-sion**.
you list more words with this sound?

on, television, _____

_____

_____

Teacher's tips

Why don't you write these spelling rules and any others you come across on a piece
of card which you laminate? This way, you can refer to them whenever you need help
with your spellings in school or at home.

9: Spelling – homophones

Homophones are words that sound the same but are spelt differently.

Sometimes you have to go back to the meaning of the word to work out the spelling; sometimes you just have to learn them!

 **Get ready**

Here are some simple homophones to choose between. Fill in the right spelling for each gap.

1 I can _____ the _____. (see/sea)

2 I _____ like to chop up some _____. (wood/would)

3 I _____ _____ pieces of cake. (ate/eight)

4 I asked _____ _____ pieces of pie. (four/for)

5 I _____ there are _____ pieces left. (know/no)

6 I _____ there were no _____ pieces left. (new/knew)

7 There's _____ much _____ do in just _____ hours. (to/two/too)

8 _____ is so much noise coming from that house of _____. (theirs/there's)

9 _____ all because of _____ size. (its/it's)

10 I can _____ the whole sound from _____. (here/hear)

Teacher's tips

A good way to remember how to spell the word **_hear_** is to remember that to do it, you must use your **ear**! Also the word **_meat_** is something you **eat**.

These homophones are a bit harder. You might have to check in your dictionary!

But this time try filling in the word class of each of the homophones. The first is done for you.

1 I will <u>break</u> my record; if I can use the <u>brake</u> on my bicycle.

Verb: <u>break</u>   Noun: <u>brake</u>

2 That's a _____ decision; I'll buy my _____ on the way home. (fair/fare)

Adjective: _____   Noun: _____

3 We had a _____ big fire; it burned in the _____. (grate/great)

Noun: _____   Adjective: _____

4 My _____ is hurting; I want it to _____ soon. (heel/heal)

Verb: _____   Noun: _____

5 We're going to _____ up soon; neither of us eats _____. (meet/meat)

Verb: _____   Noun: _____

6 I _____ seeing you; it must have been because of the _____. (missed/mist)

Verb: _____   Noun: _____

Have a go

Try writing a rhyming poem, making the lines end with your choice of these words:

_____ rain/rein/reign

_____ plain/plane

_____ main/mane

_____ vain/vein/vane

10: Spelling – common errors

One of the most common errors is doubling or not doubling the last consonant before a suffix.

So is it **taped** or **tapped**? Is it **mating** or **matting**? Actually, there's a very easy answer!

 **Get ready**

All you have to know about is short vowel sounds and long vowel sounds.

Say these words aloud, and notice the pattern of sound and spelling in each column.

	Short vowel sound	Long vowel sound
a	fat, cap, bag mat, hat	lay, stray train, rain mate, hate
e	let, men, bet pet, gen	feel, feed heal, clean Pete, gene
i	sit, tip, rib pip, din	cry, fly die, lie pipe, dine
o	pop, crop, stop rob, cop	moan, groan row, tow robe, cope
u	rut, bud, sup tub, cut	loom, loop chew, stew tube, cute

You will notice that with the long vowel sounds there are several ways of spelling the sound.

The last line of each box above is the 'magic **e**' which changes, e.g. **hat** into **hate**.

Let's practise

So now you're ready to add suffixes (like **-ing** or **-ed** or **-er**).

If the word has a short vowel sound ending in a single consonant, you double the last letter before adding the suffix, e.g. **bag**, **bagged**.

But if the word has a long vowel sound, you just add the suffix, taking off the last **-e** if there is one, e.g. **rained**, **hated**.

So pick words from the two columns on page 30, add suffixes to make new words and write them in the two jars on the right.

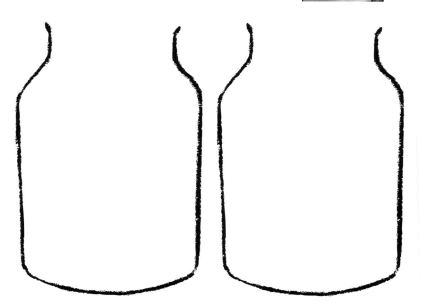

Have a go

Now let's do it in reverse; write the root words and vowel sounds for these words with suffixes:

	Root/vowel		Root/vowel
stripped	strip/short	striped	stripe/long
pinning		pining	
finned		fined	
fussing		fusing	
tapping		taping	

11: Grammar – word classes

What is a 'word class'? It is a group of words that do particular jobs in a sentence.

Nouns are names of *things*, like **cat** or **boy** or **house**.
Adjectives *describe* a noun, like **red** or **round** or **funny**.
Pronouns *stand in* for nouns, like **it** or **she** or **him**.
Verbs are *doing* words, like **swim** or **ran** or **jumping**.
Adverbs say *how* something is done, like **quickly** or **angrily**.

 **Get ready**

First, write the word class of each underlined word just above it.

1 The <u>red</u> <u>bus</u> <u>stopped</u> at the <u>lights</u>.

2 <u>It</u> <u>started</u> again after a <u>minute</u>.

3 <u>We</u> <u>jumped</u> on the <u>bus</u> at the <u>corner</u>.

4 Then <u>it</u> <u>reached</u> its <u>final</u> <u>stop</u>.

 **Let's practise**

Now let's try pronouns.
Replace the underlined nouns with pronouns.

1 <u>The red bus</u> stopped at the lights.

2 <u>My friend and I</u> jumped on <u>the bus</u> at the next stop.

3 <u>The bus</u> stopped at the corner.

4 <u>My friend and I</u> got to school late.

Next, let's focus on adverbs.

Fill in an adverb that could fit the sense of each sentence. The first is done for you.

1 Hungrily, the dragon munched his breakfast.

2 _____, he approached the little mouse.

3 _____, the mouse raced off into the grass.

4 _____, the eagle swooped overhead.

5 _____, the lion roared in the night.

Have a go

Copy out the five sentences above into one continuous paragraph, using colours for word classes:

- red for nouns • blue for adjectives • purple for pronouns • green for verbs
- orange for adverbs

_____

_____

_____

_____

_____

Teacher's tips

To remember what an **adjective**, **noun**, **verb** or **adverb** is, remember this sentence: **Adorable Nigel vaulted athletically**.

What is a sentence? Usually we say a sentence must include a verb and make complete sense; it starts with a capital letter and ends with a full stop, question mark or exclamation mark.

<u>You</u> <u>can find</u> each of those points underlined in this sentence<u>.</u>

 **Get ready**

We can make our writing more interesting by linking sentences together with **connectives**.

Choose between these **connectives** to link these pairs of sentences.

> **and**   **when**   **if**   **because**   **although**   **so**

① We set off into the rainforest _____ We had been given a detailed map.

② It felt very hot _____ The sun was behind clouds.

③ We were following the river _____ A snake crossed our path.

④ We wondered _____ It was poisonous.

⑤ We stopped _____ We trembled on the spot.

⑥ Then we looked in our guidebook _____ It had a list of poisonous snakes.

⑦ This one looked OK _____ We carried on.

⑧ We were pleased _____ We got back to the camp.

Teacher's tips

Connectives perform different functions in a sentence. For example, a connective can help to:

✳ explain the reason for something: …. because….
✳ provide a condition: ….if….
✳ provide a time: ….when….
✳ provide a contrast: ….but…. / ….although….

When you link two sentences with a connective to make one new sentence, those two parts of the new sentence are called **clauses**. Each clause still has its own verb.

Underline the verbs in these linked clauses.

1. We set off into the rainforest because we had been given a detailed map.

2. It felt very hot although the sun was behind clouds.

3. We were following the river when a snake crossed our path.

4. We wondered if it was poisonous.

5. We stopped and we trembled on the spot.

6. Then we looked in our guidebook because it had a list of poisonous snakes.

7. This one looked OK so we carried on.

8. We were pleased when we got back to the camp.

Now you try writing your own pairs of clauses, linked with these connectives:

and   when   if   because   although   so

1. _____

2. _____

3. _____

_____

_____

6. _____

13: Punctuation – commas

The comma has lots of uses:

- in a list: bread, butter, honey and jam
- to address people: Hello, my friend!
- after an adverb: Quickly, he crossed the room.
- to separate a phrase from the rest of the sentence: The last day of term, 20 July, is a Friday.
- to separate a clause from the rest of the sentence: The last day of term, which is 20 July, is a Friday.

 **Get ready**

Add commas in the right places.

1. Suddenly I dropped the jug.

2. I found the pieces on the carpet on the floor and on the staircase.

3. The last time I did such a thing last summer I was so upset.

4. This time which is even worse it was all my own fault.

5. So I'm really sorry Grandpa.

Often people put commas in the wrong places. Can you see why this sentence is wrong?

She loved her computer, she got it for Christmas.

Remember what you learnt about connectives on pages 34 and 35. This is two clauses put together without a connective! So we should rewrite it as:

She loved her computer, which she got for Christmas.

Or:

She loved her computer. She got it for Christmas.

Teacher's tips

When you write your paragraph, refer back to the rules on this page to know when to use commas. This will help you to remember where to put them.

Let's practise

Rewrite these linked clauses either with a connective or as two sentences. You choose which is better!

1. Alice frowned at the Mad Hatter, he was sitting opposite her.

   _____

   _____

2. The Mad Hatter nudged the dormouse, he was asleep.

   _____

   _____

3. The tea party was ready to begin, it was half past three.

   _____

   _____

4. They ate scones and jam, everyone loved it.

   _____

   _____

5. But who was going to clear up afterwards, they had all gone home?

   _____

   _____

Now write your own paragraph, using commas in each of the ways listed on page 36.

_____

_____

_____

14: Punctuation – apostrophes

The apostrophe looks like a flying comma, **'**, and it has just two uses:

- to mark a missing letter
- to indicate possession.

 Get ready

People started missing out letters in the most common verbs, for speed.

So, in both speech and writing, instead of **I am** we might say **I'm**, omitting the **a**. This is called a **contraction**.

Draw lines to match these contractions to their full forms.

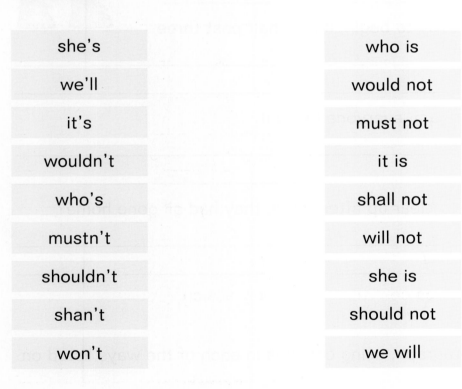

she's	who is
we'll	would not
it's	must not
wouldn't	it is
who's	shall not
mustn't	will not
shouldn't	she is
shan't	should not
won't	we will

Teacher's tips

An easy way to know where to put your apostrophe when you use it for possession is to remember that it always goes after the word that is the owner.
For example: The <u>children</u>'s toys are new. The word <u>children</u> is the owner of the toys.
The <u>boys</u>' bags are old. The word <u>boys</u> is the owner of the bags.

Let's practise

To show possession, you write an apostrophe at the end of the owner's word:

- the **owner's** cat, if there's one owner
- the **owners'** cat, if there are plural owners
- the **children's** cat, for a word that doesn't end in **s**.

Write possessive phrases for each of these:

1 Two owners have two cats *The owners' cats* _____

2 One lady has one hat _____

3 One child has two toys _____

4 Two men have two hats _____

5 Two ladies eat two cakes _____

6 Two sheep have fluffy tails _____

7 Two goats give milk _____

8 One goose lays one egg _____

Have a go

Write sentences that include contraction and possession, e.g. *She's forgotten the cat's biscuits.*

_____

_____

_____

_____

_____

15: Composition – planning

Before you start writing a long piece of **fiction**, you need to spend time planning.

What do you need to plan for fiction?

 **Get ready**

Think about:

- the genre of story (e.g. fantasy or reality)
- the theme of the story (e.g. bullying or escape)
- the setting, the characters, the plot
- the beginning, the middle and the end.

 **Let's practise**

Here's a plan for a story. Start thinking exactly what could happen in the story, ready for page 42.

Characters	Setting
A boy and a penguin	The South Pole

Beginning

They wake up one morning, side by side.

Middle

They set off for a walk together, talking about the weather.

Ending

You decide!

Teacher's tips

Spend at least 15–25 minutes planning each piece of writing. This will help you to make what you do write in the next two units as good as possible.

Before you start writing a piece of **non-fiction**, you need to plan rather different things.

What do you need to plan for non-fiction?

Think about:

- the audience (who's going to read it)
- the purpose (what you want to achieve)
- the format (printed or online; a flier, or in a journal…)
- planning your paragraphs
- planning the style of language.

Here is a plan for a poster for an event.

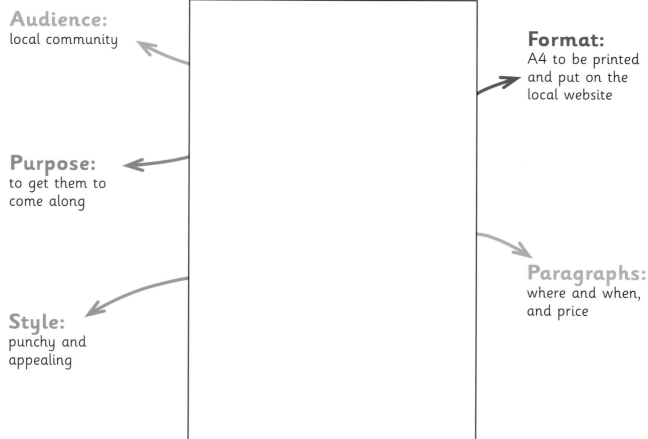

Audience:
local community

Purpose:
to get them to
come along

Style:
punchy and
appealing

Format:
A4 to be printed
and put on the
local website

Paragraphs:
where and when,
and price

Think up a possible local event, and make notes for it under the headings around poster.

Using your planning from page 40, you should be ready to write your story.

Get ready

You could try telling the story out loud to somebody. Or try writing out a couple of sentences, to help you decide on the style and the point of view.

Let's practise

When you're ready, start writing your story!

Beginning
Middle

Ending

Now, for the final stages of writing your narrative.

First, go back and edit the spellings, punctuation or anything you'd like to change.

Then, evaluate what you've written: how good is it?

You could read it aloud to somebody else, and see what they think of it.

When you're completely happy with it, you could copy it out as a final version.

Teacher's tips

When you check over your work, as well as looking at the spelling and punctuation, think about your choice of vocabulary. Could you make your language any better?

Using your planning from page 41, you should be ready to write your poster.

 **Get ready**

Check through the notes you made on the text for the poster.

Now think of a picture that could go in the middle of the poster, to attract people's attention.

Draw a rough design of the poster here, showing where the picture will go, and where you will put each part of the text.

Teacher's tips

Could you design your poster on a computer? This might help you to present it as well as possible, and will make correcting any errors easier.

Let's practise

Review your rough version, and decide what could be improved.

Now write and draw a final version of the poster.

Have a go

Now it's time to evaluate again.

Show it to other people to see what they think.

Decide what you could do better next time.

We all learn by doing things, and then trying again!

18: Composition – dialogue

Dialogue is another word for speech, or what people say.

There are several ways of laying out speech when you're writing:

- speech bubbles, as in comics
- playscripts, as we studied on pages 20 and 21
- direct speech, with speech marks.

Here is an example of speech bubbles, from the beginning of the story of *The Pied Piper*.

The characters speaking (the Mayor, two councillors and the Pied Piper) are the cast list.

Rewrite the dialogue as a playscript, checking pages 20 and 21 for the layout:

Dialogue as a playscript

_____

_____

_____

_____

_____

_____

_____

_____

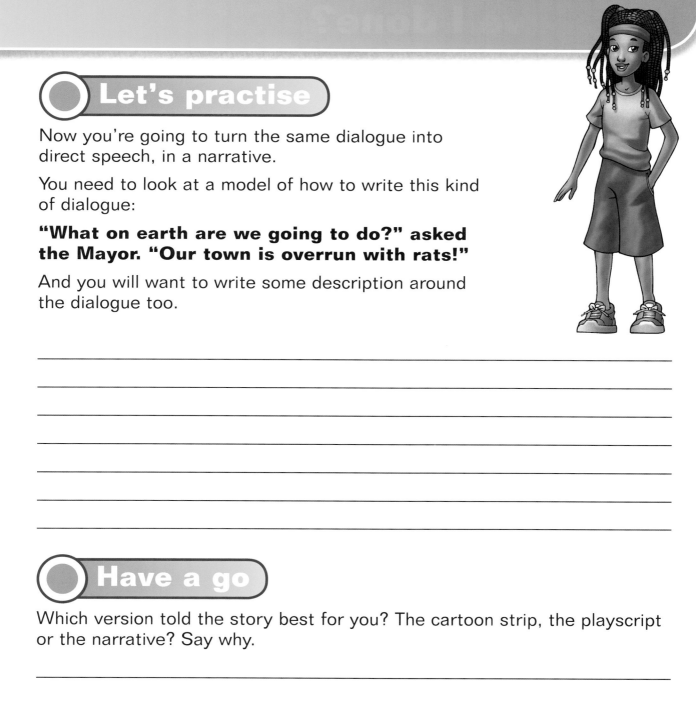

Let's practise

Now you're going to turn the same dialogue into direct speech, in a narrative.

You need to look at a model of how to write this kind of dialogue:

"What on earth are we going to do?" asked the Mayor. "Our town is overrun with rats!"

And you will want to write some description around the dialogue too.

_____

_____

_____

_____

_____

_____

_____

Have a go

Which version told the story best for you? The cartoon strip, the playscript or the narrative? Say why.

_____

_____

_____

_____

_____

Teacher's tips

Punctuating speech can be tricky. If you get stuck, have a look in a published story book for ideas or ask an adult to help you.

How have I done?

Comprehension

List some distinctive features for each of these genres of text:

Poetry _____

_____

Fiction _____

_____

Playscript _____

_____

Information text _____

_____

Handwriting

What are the five kinds of join?

_____

_____

_____

_____

_____

Spelling

What is a prefix? _____

_____

What is a suffix? _____

_____

What is a homophone? _____

_____

Add **-er** to the end of **fat**, **thin**, **slim** and **tall**:

_____

_____

Grammar

Write the word class of each underlined word:

The <u>quick</u> brown <u>fox</u> <u>jumps</u> <u>over</u> the lazy dog.

_____

_____

Underline the main clause in this sentence:

The brown fox enjoys jumping, especially over lazy dogs.

Punctuation

Add commas to this sentence where they are needed:

The brown fox who is quicker than the lazy dog enjoys jumping.

Add apostrophes to this sentence where they are needed:

The foxs bark is harsher than the dogs bark.

Composition

Punctuate this piece of dialogue:

Lie still said the fox Im thinking of practising my jumping

The dog was so lazy he just yawned YAWN

_____

_____

_____

_____

Writing and Punctuation

- **Master the key skills**
- **Write and punctuate with confidence**

Here's a list that Megan wrote. It lists all her favourite things in life. They are all the things she'd save if there was a flood!

My pink boots
My old teddy bear
My gran's photo
My first tooth
My black mouse
My diary
Big bottle of water for survival
My mobile
My purple pen
The chocolate cake from my last birthday party

Get ready

1 Do you use capital letters in this kind of list?

_____

2 Do you use punctuation in this kind of list?

_____

3 When do you start a new line in a list?

_____

Let's practise

Now write a list of the ten things you'd save, if you knew a mega-disaster was coming!

Never mind if some of them are a bit difficult to pack . . .

1 _____

2 _____

3 _____

4 _____

5 _____

6 _____

7 _____

8 _____

9 _____

10 _____

Have a go

Go and ask other people in your family what they'd save, and make lists for each of them.

Teacher's tips

There are no trick questions here! Just look at the list to answer questions 1–3 in **Get ready.** Will you pack things that you treasure or things that will help you survive? Use the example list to help your own writing.

2: Write a recipe

A recipe is a kind of **instruction**, which tells you how to make something.

It's often a recipe for cooking, but it might be for making something else.

Here's a recipe that's really different.

How to make your mum happy

<u>You will need:</u>

1 piece of card   1 tray   Your mum's favourite food and drink

<u>What to do:</u>

1 Fold the card and draw a picture on the front.
2 Write a message inside, telling your mum what a great person she is.
3 Find a tray in the kitchen, or a very strong piece of board.
4 Pile on her favourite food and drink.
5 Find a good moment when she's sitting down.
6 Give her the tray and your card as a big surprise.
7 Last of all, give her a big kiss!

Get ready

What are the headings for the two parts of the instruction?

1 _____

2 _____

Let's practise

Now think up your own idea for a recipe in life.

It could be how to make your best friend happy, or it could be how to make a really awful mess!

<u>You will need:</u>

_____

_____

_____

<u>What to do:</u>

1 _____

2 _____

3 _____

4 _____

 ## Have a go

Write down the recipe for cooking your favourite food.

First list the things you need, then list the things you do to make the dish. Make your instructions as clear as possible.

Teacher's tips

Look back at the recipe you are given as an example on page 54 to help you come up with ideas and remember – there's no right answer. Just use your imagination!

3: Write directions

Another kind of instruction tells someone how to get somewhere.

This is called giving **directions**, and it helps if you have a map to work from.

Here are the directions that Little Red Riding Hood's mother gave her to reach her grandmother's house in the woods.

Leave the house behind you, and walk straight on for half a mile.
When you come to the big oak tree, turn right.
Walk on another half a mile until you come to the stream.
Cross the bridge, and turn left.
When you reach the ruined farm, turn right.
Grandmother's house is then straight in front of you.

Draw a line on the picture to show where Little Red Riding Hood had to go. Start from the house at the bottom.

Let's practise

Write the directions that Grandmother would have given Little Red Riding Hood to get back home. That is, if she hadn't been eaten by the wolf . . .

_____

_____

_____

_____

_____

_____

_____

_____

_____

_____

Have a go

Write directions for your best friend, telling him or her how to get from school to your home. You could draw a map as well, if it helps.

Teacher's tips

Look carefully at the picture. Then read the directions. Place your direction line for each part of the journey, in turn. Check that your direction lines start in the bottom left of the picture and end in the top right.

4: Write a definition

When do you use a dictionary?

A dictionary is really useful for checking your spelling, and for finding out what words mean.

The meaning of a word is also called a **definition**.

Read the definitions below. Fill in the word you think each definition is describing on the first line.

_____ a large monster with wings, that you read about in stories _____

_____ a very big piece of ice floating in the sea _____

_____ a word describing the taste of nuts _____

_____ a person whose job is to fit and mend water pipes and taps _____

_____ to go backwards in a car _____

Get ready

1. Look up the words in your own dictionary. Which definition do you prefer: the one above or the one in your dictionary?

2. Now write **noun**, **verb** or **adjective** after each word. Your dictionary may tell you this.

Let's practise

Now try writing your own definitions for these words:

deckchair _____

_____

haunted _____

_____

magnet _____

_____

nose _____

_____

rise _____

_____

sword _____

_____

wand _____

_____

Have a go

Play a game reading definitions from the dictionary and asking your friends to guess what the words are.

Teacher's tips

Remember a **noun** is a naming word, a **verb** is a doing word and an **adjective** is a describing word. A **noun** can be a *person, place, thing* or *idea* and an **adjective** describes a noun!

5: Write an advert

How do you persuade someone that they'd like what you like?

You have to be very good with words to describe something so that you make someone else want to try it too.

Take your favourite food, for instance – how can you turn a yummy taste into the kind of description that makes your best friend beg for a bite?

WHEN YOU'VE CRUNCHED
THROUGH THE MUNCHY BIT,
AND SUCKED UP THE SOFTY BIT,
THE RICH BIT IN THE MIDDLE
IS THE MELTING CHOCOLATE CENTRE
OF THE PERFECT CHOCOLATE DOUGHNUT.
IT'S A CHOCOHOLIC'S DREAM COME TRUE!

Find a highlighter pen, and mark each word in the advert that really tempts you.

Let's practise

Describe your favourite food, and draw a picture, to make us all want a taste.

Have a go

Invent a new toy, and write an advert persuading parents to buy it for their children. Draw a picture, too, if you like.

Teacher's tips

Remember to use exciting **adjectives**. Words like *yummy*, *scrumptious* and *delicious* might help! If you want to make your advert even better why not try some creative **verbs** and some **alliteration**? For example, *Try **munching** this **perfect** pepperoni pizza!*

61

6: Write a questionnaire

Do you like asking questions? If so, you could try writing a questionnaire for friends and family to fill in.

Here's one that Megan wrote, with the answers she got from her granny.

What is your name?	Granny Ross
What is your favourite food?	Baked beans
What is your favourite colour?	Purple
Where was your favourite holiday?	Wales
Who is your favourite singer?	Billy Fury
What is your favourite animal?	Giraffe
What are your favourite shoes?	My fur boots
What time do you go to bed?	Never before 10 o'clock

Get ready

1   List the question words used at the start of the sentences.

_____

2   What is put at the end of each question? _____

3   What punctuation is used in the answers? _____

Let's practise

Now write your own questionnaire, for your friends or family.

You could add lots of different questions, like: What is the earliest thing you can remember happening to you?

_____

_____

_____

_____

_____

_____

_____

_____

Have a go

Make copies of your questionnaire, if you can, so you can ask lots of different people to fill in their answers.

Teacher's tips

If you have difficulty coming up with questions for your questionnaire, use the example provided on page 62 to help you. And remember, make questions relevant for your audience. *What's your favourite bedtime story* might not be the best question to ask your gran!

When do we write letters? When we want to tell someone something, and maybe when we don't know someone well enough to telephone or text.

Have you ever written to an author, to tell them how much you like their book?

This is the letter I typed to Robert Swindells to tell him how much I enjoyed reading his book *Ice Palace*.

---

26 Sunny Terrace
Chelmsford CO5 9AH

26 August 2007

Dear Mr Swindells,

I'd like to tell you how much I enjoyed reading Ice Palace.

I found the whole book a wonderful fantasy story, which made me feel really scared, as well as wanting to read on to the end.

The bit I especially liked was when Ivan was stuck in the cave, and searching for his brother.

Thank you for writing this book. I shall try to find more of your stories in our library.

Yours sincerely,
Amina Desai

Can you find all these parts of the letter? Draw lines to link them to the text above.

1 Home address   **2** Date   **3** Greeting

4 Message   **5** Ending

Let's practise

Write a letter to your favourite author.
Tell them which is your favourite book
of theirs, why you liked the book
overall, what your favourite bit was,
and what you might read next.

Have a go

Write a letter to your local library, asking them to stock a book you've really enjoyed.

Teacher's tips

Make sure you lay out your letter correctly. If you're writing to an author, you'll need to be extra careful with your spelling and punctuation.

8: Explain in words

I'm fascinated by how things are made, or how things get to where they are.

We often use pictures or diagrams to show how these things happen.

Can you see what the pictures below are telling us?

Get ready

1. Talk through what's happening in the pictures, as if the person you're talking to doesn't understand them.

2. Did you notice which tense you were using? Was it the present tense or the past tense?

Let's practise

Now write down your explanation in words.

Use the numbered stages to help you.

1 _____

_____

2 _____

_____

3 _____

_____

4 _____

_____

5 _____

_____

6 _____

_____

Have a go

Write out the explanation of how something else is made.

Try drawing the pictures as well, if you can.

Teacher's tips

It might help you when it comes to **Let's practise** to look back at each picture and say out loud what each picture shows. For example, you might say *Cows eat grass* for picture 1. Then write this down.

Do you ever read newspapers, to read **reports** of things that have happened?

If the report describes the events in the order that they happened, it is called a **chronological report**.

Look at the newspaper report below, which describes an escape from a zoo.

PYTHON ESCAPES!

Fear and panic swept the town of Marwick as a mountain python escaped from its cage.

The keepers first noticed it was missing at dawn, when they went round with morning feeds. They raised the alarm, and local police were given instructions on how to corner the snake, if anyone reported a sighting.

Early in the day the local school reported a possible sighting, but the zoo were not sure if they believed the stripy creature spotted in the playground really was the python.

Residents at an old people's home then thought they'd seen something slithery, but again it disappeared before the police could follow it.

In the end the zoo found the python in the farm area, where it had eaten all the rabbits and mice. So maybe it had never got out into the town at all.

Get ready

1 What tense is the main report written in, the past tense or the present tense? _____

2 Can you spot all the words that mark the sequence of time (connecting words), at the beginning of each paragraph?
Mark them with a highlighter pen.

Let's practise

Now write a newspaper report of a dramatic incident in your home town.

Use the past tense, and use connecting words at the beginning of each paragraph, to stress the sequence of time.

Write a report for your school newspaper or school website, describing an event that happened at school.

Teacher's tips

Read the first sentence of each paragraph in turn. This will help you spot the *time words*. Examples of such words are *then, first, at midday, next* and so on. If you are stuck for ideas in **Let's practise**, make something up!

Suppose you wanted to respond to that newspaper article about the python escaping. Imagine you thought the zoo should think more about safety in your school and neighbourhood. Here's the kind of letter you might write.

Primrose School
Princess Road
Marwick MAR 6JL

1 October 2007

Dear Marwick Zoo,

We were worried to read in the local newspaper that one of your pythons might have escaped last week.

We kept thinking we'd seen it in the playground, so we were very scared.

We think it's important for the local neighbourhood to feel safe, so we hope that you have enough guards to make sure your animals don't escape.

We'd like to hear more about how your zoo is run.

Yours sincerely,
Class 4B

1. Compare this letter with the one in Unit 7. Which features do this letter and the one in Unit 7 have in common?

_____

2. What were the class worried about?

_____

3. How did they make the letter end on a positive note?

_____

 **Let's practise**

Now write your own letter to the zoo, expressing a different point of view. Maybe you think they shouldn't be keeping pythons there at all. Make sure you lay out the letter in the same way as the one from Class 4B.

 **Have a go**

Look through your local newspaper for reports that make you want to respond. Write a letter to the newspaper giving your point of view.

Teacher's tips

Remember, when you write your letter in response to the newspaper article in Unit 9, to be polite. At the same time as saying what you think, why not give reasons for why you think this?

11: Write a playscript

Do you know what a playscript is?

A **playscript** is how we write out the words that people speak in a play.

Look at this example, and read the different speeches out loud.

[*The* MAYOR *is sitting with his* COUNCILLORS.]

MAYOR: What on earth are we going to do? Our town is overrun with rats!

1st COUNCILLOR: There are rats in the cellars!

2nd COUNCILLOR: There are rats in the streets!

[*Enter a young man, dressed in red and yellow.*]

PIED PIPER: Please, sirs. I think I can help you.

MAYOR: How can you do that?

PIED PIPER: I know a charm that makes animals follow me.

MAYOR: And how do you do that?

PIED PIPER: I play on this pipe, and the animals follow.

MAYOR: That's wonderful! What should we pay you?

PIED PIPER: [*Modestly*] I'd like a thousand gilders, please.

MAYOR: We'll give you fifty thousand gilders, sir!

Now match each of these features to the script above, by drawing lines to examples in the text.

1. Name of the person speaking, in capitals

2. Words the people say, in ordinary type

3. Stage directions, in square brackets and italics

Let's practise

Try writing a part of a playscript.

You could choose a well-known folk tale, like the one here. Or you could use a story you make up yourself.

Include all the features from the example opposite. You will need to continue on a separate piece of paper.

_____

_____

_____

_____

_____

_____

_____

_____

_____

Have a go

Act out your playscript with a group of friends.

Teacher's tips

If you have difficulty coming up with ideas for your playscript, you could always base your script on something you have seen on television. With such a short script, it's best to stick to only two or three characters.

12: Punctuate speech

In the last unit, we looked at how to write speech in a play.
If you are writing speech in a cartoon strip or in a story, you do it differently.
Below, we're going to show you the same story of the Pied Piper, first as a cartoon, and then as a story.

The Mayor was sitting with his Councillors, and he was very worried.
"What on earth are we going to do?" he asked. "Our town is overrun with rats!"
"There are rats in the cellars!" said the First Councillor.
"There are rats in the streets!" echoed the Second Councillor.
At that point a young man came in, dressed in red and yellow.
"Please, sirs," he said softly. "I think I can help you."
The Mayor was amazed. "How can you do that?" he asked.
"I know a charm that makes animals follow me," said the Piper.

 **Get ready**

When do you use speech marks to show the words people speak?
Mark with a tick (✓) or a cross (✗).

1 Playscript ☐   **2** Speech bubbles ☐   **3** Story ☐

Let's practise

Take the playscript you wrote in Unit 11.

Write it out as a story, using the model opposite for how to do the speech marks. Look at the model carefully – it's quite fiddly, putting the speech marks and the other punctuation in the right places. You will need to continue on a separate piece of paper.

Have a go

Draw the same conversation as a cartoon with speech bubbles.

Teacher's tips

Here's a useful tip for **Let's practise**: whenever a new person speaks, take a new line. Also, notice what has happened to the directions from the playscript in the story. Remember to do this with your own story.

Can you describe someone so that your reader can really picture him or her?

Can you make your reader either want to meet the person or run a mile?

You have to describe all the little details of what people look like and how they might behave, if you are to make your reader really believe in them!

Here is a **character sketch**.

I saw someone walking their dog this morning.

At least, first I just saw the dog-lead in the gap of our front hedge. So I started to imagine who was on each end of the dog-lead, before I caught a full picture of the two of them.

It was the dog I saw first. He was one of those pit bull terriers who look rather scary, but are probably quite amiable really. He had big square shoulders, and rather turned-out feet.

He was moving slowly, as if he was not out for a walk so much as ambling out to inspect the neighbourhood. He had slitty eyes, as if he hadn't quite woken up yet.

So it wasn't such a surprise when the owner then appeared in the next gap of the hedge. He was slow on his feet too. And his toes turned out too. He wasn't menacing at all, more just a sleepy character who liked to look a bit more frightening than he really was. I then remembered that I'd seen them both in the park, the dog asleep on the ground with his legs splayed out, and the man asleep on a bench, in the middle of the afternoon.

They left me thinking: which came first, the man or the dog?

Get ready

1   Read the character sketch, and use a highlighter pen to mark the bits you think the writer has done best.

2   Are there any words you don't know? Either try guessing what they mean, or look them up in a dictionary.

Let's practise

Try writing your own character sketch of a dog and its owner. Really try to picture them in your head. Don't forget to use lots of details to describe their appearance, and what this suggests about how they might behave.

_____

_____

_____

_____

_____

_____

_____

_____

_____

Have a go

Look for a photo in a magazine of someone whose life you'd like to imagine. Try writing a day-in-the-life of your character.

Teacher's tips

Having a picture of a person in front of you as you write a character sketch helps. Try this. Also, brainstorming some useful describing words on rough paper before you write your sketch will make your writing even better.

14: Describe a setting

Where do stories happen? Where would you like to make a story of yours happen?

You need to use lots of adjectives to describe your setting, so that your reader can picture it exactly.

Deep in a dark black space. Dank and dark, bleak and black. Is there any light at all? Yes, there's a piercing white light ahead: could it be the mouth of a cave, or the light at the end of a tunnel? It's a tiny relief compared with this overwhelming blackness, this damp chilling darkness, enveloping everything. What are the sounds? A drip of moisture from the roof, falling into a puddle in the rough ground underfoot. But otherwise there is just silence, leaving me nothing to hear, as well as nothing to see. Where on earth am I?

Get ready

1 Highlight all the adjectives in the description above.

2 Do you think the description is effective? _____

_____

Let's practise

Now it's your turn to describe a setting.
Will you make it obvious where it is?
Or will you leave your reader guessing?
Don't forget your adjectives, and
think of all the senses you use: sight,
hearing, touch, taste and smell.

_____

_____

_____

_____

_____

_____

_____

_____

_____

Again, try looking through a magazine, this time to find somewhere gorgeous you'd like to go on holiday. Describe what you think the place would be like.

Teacher's tips

A good way to start your description of a setting is *As I look around me I notice....*
Other sentence starts that might help are:
I hear ....
The smell of ......drifts towards me.
I stretch my hand out and feel ....

15: Plan a story

Now you can start to plan a whole story, using your character in your setting. (Or choose a new character in a new setting.)

What's going to happen? You need a **beginning**, a **middle** and an **ending** to make your plot work. Look at the plan below.

Character	Setting
Man and dog	Dark tunnel

Beginning

They wake up

Middle

They realise where they are

Ending

They walk to safety

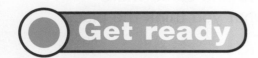

Would you plan your character and your setting completely before you begin to plan your plot? Or do you think they might develop while you are writing?

Let's practise

Fill in the boxes below to plan your own story.

When you come to write your story, you will write a paragraph each for the **beginning**, **middle** and **ending**.

Character
_____

Setting
_____

Beginning

_____

_____

Middle

_____

_____

Ending

_____

_____

Have a go

When you are ready, get a separate piece of paper and write your story. This is just your rough draft. You will write your final version a bit later . . .

Teacher's tips

A good story plan will have a bit of drama in it. In the example plan the dark tunnel provides drama and excitement. Try to include some excitement in your plan too.

16: Punctuate your story

In the last unit we planned our stories, and you went off to write a rough version of your whole plot.

Here's what we wrote for the three paragraphs of our plot.

The man woke up slowly. Where on earth was he? It was pitch black, and rather damp. At least the dog was still at his feet; that was something. But what were they doing here?
He stroked his dog's familiar fur, to stop himself trembling with panic.

"Come on, boy," he said. "We've got to get out of here."
They headed towards the source of light, stumbling through the puddles.
"If only the dog could talk," he thought. "He could remind me how we got in here."
They headed forwards, the man keeping one hand on the side of the tunnel for safety. The shape of the light got bigger and bigger, in the shape of a growing white 'n'.

At last they broke into the daylight. They were on the bank of a little canal, which snaked round the hillside to bring water to all the crops. They had been inside one of the tunnels the canal flowed through, and the man must have fallen or passed out while they were in the tunnel. Never again! He would make sure he never walked through dark tunnels again for the rest of his life!

When you've read the story, have a look at the punctuation.

1 Does every sentence start with a capital letter and end with either a full stop, a question mark or an exclamation mark? Mark them all in red.

2 Has the author used commas to separate a list, or to help the reader pause in the middle of a sentence? Mark the commas in blue.

3 Has the author used any semi-colons and colons in the middle of sentences for longer pauses? Mark them in pink.

4 Has the author used speech marks correctly for speech? Mark them in green.

Let's practise

Now you can 'edit' your rough version of your story, by checking the four punctuation questions in **Get ready**.

When you are ready, copy out a final version of your story into the space below. You may need to continue on a separate piece of paper.

Have a go

Try writing a longer story, of more than three paragraphs. You could then make it into a folded book, with a proper cover, and give it to someone in your family as a present.

Teacher's tips

If you need some help with punctuation, you can always ask for help from a grown-up. The most difficult bit will be punctuating speech. Look in books that you have read to see how this is done.

17: Write a different ending

Do you remember the setting and characters we brought together in Unit 15?

Well, maybe there's a different explanation of how the man and his dog got into the tunnel, and how they'll get out!

Here's a spider diagram with lots of different possibilities.

The dog had attacked him

Ghosts

Railway tunnel

Sea cliffs

The train approaches

It's all a bad dream

Get ready

Mark the spider diagram with ticks (✓), crosses (✗) and question marks (?) to indicate how you feel about each possibility.

Which option was your favourite?

Or would you choose something entirely different from your own imagination?

Write a different ending to the story, to make it more exciting for you. You may need to continue on a separate piece of paper.

_____

_____

_____

_____

_____

_____

_____

_____

 **Have a go**

Take a well-known story, and write a completely different ending for it.

Does your ending make the story better?

Teacher's tips

When you **Have a go,** you could always try out a *funny ending* or an *unexpected ending*. Maybe you could even have a *mysterious ending*?

18: Write a poem

Write a whole poem myself! How scary does that sound?

Actually there are lots of ways of making it less scary. One way is to work from a 'model'. This means you look at the form or shape of someone else's poem, and use it as a 'prompt' to write your own. And that's quite all right – it's not cheating.

So, read aloud the poem below.

My Week at School

On Monday we did pottery,
On Tuesday we did craft;
On Wednesday we did sums and things,
On Thursday we just laughed.
On Friday we did question marks,
And What and Why and Who,
But now that it's the weekend
I can choose just what I'll do!

Which lines rhyme? Number the lines, and draw lines to link the ones that rhyme.

Let's practise

Try using the same idea, of the days of the week, to write your own poem.

Look out for which lines have to rhyme!

On Monday _____

On Tuesday _____

On Wednesday _____

On Thursday _____

On Friday _____

_____

_____

_____

Have a go

Try using times of day, or the months of the year, as a way of shaping some more poems.

Teacher's tips

Remember, a **rhyme** happens when the end sounds in two words sound the same. The words *see* and *three* rhyme. When you write your own poem, say lines aloud to help you rhyme them.

19: Write a shape poem

Do you like shape poems? I love reading them, but I've never tried writing one before.

One way of doing it is to draw the shape of a country or continent and then, inside the shape, write all the words that the place makes you think of.

Here's one on Africa, for instance.

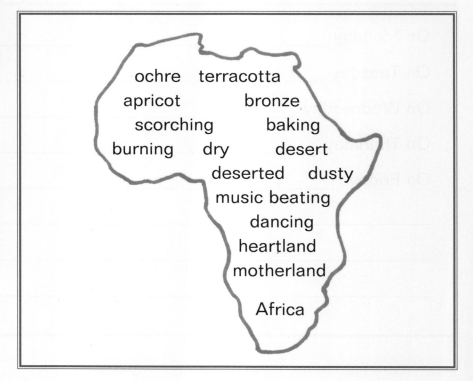

ochre   terracotta
apricot   bronze
scorching   baking
burning   dry   desert
         deserted   dusty
         music beating
              dancing
             heartland
           motherland

              Africa

What colours does this poem make you think of? Colour in the shape with the right kind of colours.

Now write a shape poem of your own. It doesn't have to be about a country; it could be about a food, or a building, or a person. Draw the outline shape first, and then fill it with words that the shape makes you think of.

Write shape poems for a whole jungle full of wild animals!

Teacher's tips

There are a few colour words in the Africa poem which you may not know! Look up the words *terracotta, ochre, apricot* and *bronze* in a dictionary. When you write your poem, use a range of **adjectives**, **nouns** and **verbs**.

20: Write a haiku

Now let's try a **haiku**.

A haiku has three lines, with the middle line longer than the first and last.

Here are some examples.

a

An old pond
The sound of a frog jumping
Into water.

b

First day of school
Toes cramped and blistered red
From new school shoes.

c

Last day of term
Classroom chairs looking forward to
Weeks of peace.

How many syllables are there in each line of the three haiku above? Many haiku have five, seven and five syllables in their three lines, but not all haiku follow this pattern.

Let's practise

Now try writing your own haiku.

Haiku are often about the seasons, so
that might help to get you started.

_____

_____

_____

_____

_____

_____

_____

_____

_____

Have a go

One author has recently tried condensing the plots of major novels into
haiku. Could you do this for your favourite novel?

Teacher's tips

Remember a **syllable** is a one beat sound in a word. If you tapped out each beat in
the word _tomorrow_ (to-mo-rrow) you would hear that it has three syllables. The word
cramped has only one syllable, however.

How have I done?

Quiz on writing

Can you remember which special features you'd find in these different kinds of writing?

Draw lines to match them up.

What you need:	Instructions
Turn left.	Character sketch
Address and date	Questionnaire
What's your name?	Speech
PIED PIPER:	Playscript
[*He came in slowly*.]	Recipe
"Too right," he said.	Directions
Poem of three lines	Setting
He was a burly man.	Haiku
It was a dark and stormy night.	Letter

Careful! It's not necessarily one feature per kind of writing . . .

Quiz on punctuation

Each of these lines has an error of punctuation.

Write out the correct version on the line below.

1 "All right" said the clown.

_____

2 I'll take all these the ball the ring and the crown.

_____

3 The bird, which was sitting on the line sang the loudest.

_____

4 How on earth can I handle all that.

_____

5 "Are we going to school?" She asked.

_____

6 William said. "It's just as well."

_____

7 You take the shortest; We'll take the longest.

_____

8 It's about time too, I replied.

_____

9 Those were the days she said, with a sigh.

_____

10 And that's all for now I'm afraid.

_____

Teacher's tips

The **special features** are on the left and the **types of writing** are on the right. To match the **feature** 'Turn left' in the left hand column, draw a line to the **type of writing** 'Directions' in the right hand column.

Maths

- **Build understanding**
- **Master the core skills**

1: Numbers to 1000

We have a very clever way of writing numbers. Using just the digits 0, 1, 2, 3, 4, 5, 6, 7, 8 and 9 we can write any numbers we like.

The important thing to remember is **where** each digit is placed in the number.

Let's look at the number **254**.

Th	H	T	U
	2	5	4

The 2 in this number is worth **2 hundreds** or **200**.
The 5 in this number is worth **5 tens** or **50**.
The 4 in this number is worth **4 units (or ones)** or **4**.

● Get ready

The numbers below are all written with the digits 3, 7 and 8.

Write what each digit in the numbers is worth.

One has been done for you.

1 378   <u>300</u>   <u>70</u>   <u>8</u>

2 873   ____   ____   _

3 387   ____   ____   _

4 738   ____   ____   _

5 783   ____   ____   _

6 837   ____   ____   _

Now write the six blue numbers above in order, starting with the smallest.

_____378_____ _____ _____ _____ _____ _____

Let's practise

When ordering numbers like these, compare the hundreds digits first, as they are worth more.
Then compare the tens digits and then the units digits.

Order these numbers, smallest first.

7 382, 503, 254, 199 _____

8 442, 244, 242, 424 _____

9 99, 101, 321, 309 _____

10 63, 603, 306, 360 _____

Continue these sequences by counting on in 100s, 10s or 1s.

11 127, 227, 327, 427, _____, _____, _____

12 348, 358, 368, 378, _____, _____, _____

13 409, 509, 609, 709, _____, _____, _____

14 586, 587, 588, 589, _____, _____, _____

15 276, 286, 296, 306, _____, _____, _____

16 78, 88, 98, 108, _____, _____, _____

Have a go

Write down the last three digits of your telephone number.
Use each digit once to make a 3-digit number less than 1000.
How many different numbers can you make?

Write them in order from largest to smallest.

_____

Teacher's tips

Say numbers aloud and add 'sets of' between each number to help partition into hundreds, tens and units. So 542 is read: five (sets of) hundred, four (sets of) 'ty', and two (units). Think of 'ty' as meaning '10'.

2: Counting in multiples

If you start at zero and count up in equal-sized steps you create a sequence of **multiples**.

For example, if you count on in steps of 3 from zero you get:

3, 6, 9, 12, 15, 18, 21, 24, 27, 30, 33, 36...

These are **multiples of 3**.

If you count on in steps of 5 from zero you get:

5, 10, 15, 20, 25, 30, 35, 40, 45, 50, 55, 60...

These are **multiples of 5**.

⬤ Get ready

Count on from zero to create a sequence of multiples.

1 Count in steps of 2.

2 __ __ __ __ __ __ __ __ __ __

2 Count in steps of 4.

4 __ __ __ __ __ __ __ __ __ __

3 Count in steps of 10.

10 __ __ __ __ __ __ __ __ __ __

Let's practise

Count on from zero to create a sequence of multiples.

4 Count in steps of 8.

  8 __ __ __ __ __ __ __ __ __ __

5 Count in steps of 50.

  50 __ __ __ __ __ __ __ __ __ __

6 Count in steps of 100.

  100 ___ ___ ___ ___ ___ ___ ___ ___ ___ ___

Fill in the missing numbers in each sequence of multiples.

7 3, 6, 9, 12, _____, 18, 21, _____, 27, _____, 33, _____

8 5, _____, 15, 20, _____, _____, 35, _____, 45, 50, _____, 60

9 50, 100, _____, _____, 250, 300, _____, 400, 450, _____

10 8, 16, _____, 32, 40, _____, 56, _____, 72, _____

Have a go

Use a calculator to explore some other
sequences of multiples.
Keep adding the same number to create
a sequence.
Try finding the multiples of 25 or 11.
What patterns do you notice?

Teacher's tips
Add the digits of a 2-digit number – if the answer is a multiple of 3 then the original number is also a multiple of 3, if the answer is 9 then the original number is also a multiple of 9.

3: Addition and subtraction facts

It is important to be able to add and subtract numbers quickly and easily in your head.

Addition grid

+	1	5	3	2	4
6	7	11	9	8	10
9	10	14	12	11	13
7	8	12	10	9	11
8	9	13	11	10	12

Subtraction grid

−	1	5	3	2	4
6	5	1	3	4	2
9	8	4	6	7	5
7	6	2	4	5	3
8	7	3	5	6	4

Addition and subtraction grids can help you to practise the facts. For addition, add the number at the top of each column to the number at the left-hand end of each row.

For subtraction, subtract the number at the top of each column from the number at the left-hand end of each row.

Get ready

1 Complete the addition and subtraction grids.

+	5	8	7
6			
9			
5			
7			
8			

−	5	3	7
10			
8			
9			
11			
7			

Let's practise

2 Complete the addition and subtraction grids.

+	9	5	8
13			
18			
11			
24			
35			

−	8	4	7
20			
13			
16			
22			
19			

3 The grids below involve adding and subtracting 2-digit numbers. It might help you to add the tens digits and units/ones digits separately, like this.

24 + 17   = 20 + 10 + 4 + 7
**   =   30   +   11   = 41**

+	11	17	14
21			
15			
28			
39			
18			

−	11	16	19
49			
36			
25			
21			
32			

Have a go

Draw your own addition or subtraction grid and see how quickly you can fill in the answers.

Teacher's tips

It often helps to lay out problems with the two numbers above each other so you can add/subtract the units, then the tens. Or use a number line/number square to count on (addition) or count back (subtraction).

When adding or subtracting numbers in your head it is important to remember the place value of each digit.

For example, when adding 100 to 328, you add 1 to the hundreds digit to give the answer 428.

Th	H	T	U
	3	2	8
+	1	0	0
	4	2	8

When subtracting 10 from 328, you take 1 from the tens digit to give the answer 318.

Th	H	T	U
	3	2	8
–		1	0
	3	1	8

Get ready

Answer these addition questions.

1. 382 + 10 = _____

2. 173 + 10 = _____

3. 493 + 1 = _____

4. 638 + 10 = _____

5. 912 + 1 = _____

6. 825 + 100 = _____

7. 244 + 10 = _____

8. 307 + 100 = _____

9. 894 + 1 = _____

10. 581 + 100 = _____

11. 367 + 1 = _____

12. 789 + 10 = _____

Write out these questions in columns and answer them using a written method.

7 624 − 395

10 583 − 268

8 872 − 393

11 830 − 481

9 708 − 519

12 804 − 439

 Have a go

If you find this type of sum difficult you can always work them out by moving along a number line.

Look at how Alfie works out 381 − 158.

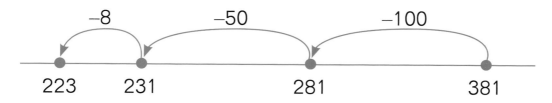

−8   −50   −100

223   231   281   381

Try using both methods and see which way you find quicker!

Teacher's tips

'Borrowing' is temporarily changing the way a number is written to make solving a problem easier. By 'splitting up' a set of numbers (e.g. 10 into ten units) we're not changing the value of the number, just how it's written.

7: Word problems

When solving problems, read each question carefully and decide what you will do. For example whether to add, subtract, multiply or divide.

After you have decided what to do, you should make an approximation. This will give you a rough idea of the answer.

Then calculate and finally check your answer with your approximation to see if it is sensible.

When you write the final answer, remember to give the correct unit, such as £, p, cm, kg, l, m, g, etc.

Get ready

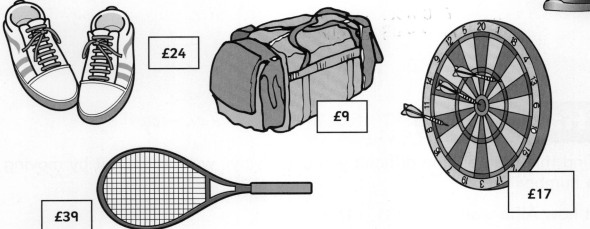

£24

£9

£17

£39

1 Kim buys a sports bag and a pair of trainers. How much do they cost altogether? _____

2 Megan has £50. She buys a tennis racquet. How much change does she get? _____

3 Alfie's mum buys two pairs of trainers, one pair for Alfie and one for his brother. She also buys a dartboard for them. How much does she pay? _____

4 Abbie buys a sports bag, a dartboard and a tennis racquet. How much change from £100 does she get? _____

Let's practise

When prices are given in both pounds and pence, be careful not to mix them up. Change the prices so that they are all the same unit.

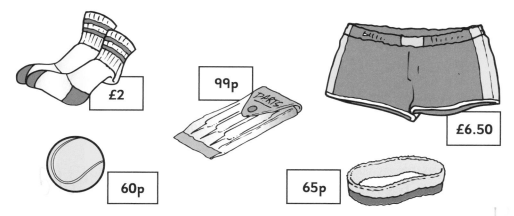

£2   99p   £6.50

60p   65p

5. Charlie buys a sports bag (see price on the opposite page) and a tennis ball. How much do they cost altogether? _____

6. Amina pays with a £10 note. She buys a pack of darts and a pair of shorts. How much change does she get? _____

7. Jamelia buys two tennis balls, a pair of socks and a sweatband. How much is that in total? _____

8. Alfie buys a tennis racquet (see price on the opposite page) and a sweatband. How much change from £50 is he given? _____

9. Charlie's dad spent exactly £23.50 on buying two of the items shown. Which two items did he buy?

_____ and _____

Have a go

Find out how much it costs to buy clothes and equipment for your favourite game or sport. Imagine you had £100 to spend. What would you buy?

Teacher's tips

When solving word problems it can help to translate them into a number sentence by writing the values and actions above the word problem. Think carefully about what the actions are to write the number sentence in the correct order.

8: Times tables

How well do you know your times tables? By now you should know the facts for the 2, 3, 4, 5, and 10 times tables.

A multiplication tables grid can help you keep a check of which facts you're sure of.

Multiply the number in the left hand column by the number at the top of each column.

1 Fill in the answers to check how well you know your 2, 3, 4, 5 and 10 times tables. Try them out of order, by choosing any box to fill in.

×	2	3	4	5	10
1	2				
2					
3					
4					
5					
6					
7					
8					
9					
10					
11					
12					

Check and mark your answers. Colour all the correct answers yellow and the wrong answers red.

Let's practise

2 Answer these questions as quickly as you can.

5 × 1 = _____	3 × 3 = _____	8 × 3 = _____
6 × 5 = _____	12 × 4 = _____	9 × 5 = _____
8 × 2 = _____	2 × 11 = _____	10 × 12 = _____
5 × 3 = _____	7 × 5 = _____	4 × 0 = _____
2 × 10 = _____	8 × 4 = _____	4 × 6 = _____
8 × 4 = _____	4 × 9 = _____	3 × 12 = _____
4 × 4 = _____	1 × 10 = _____	5 × 0 = _____
3 × 9 = _____	5 × 5 = _____	6 × 3 = _____
10 × 3 = _____	12 × 5 = _____	1 × 3 = _____
11 × 3 = _____	7 × 4 = _____	3 × 4 = _____
5 × 9 = _____	7 × 3 = _____	10 × 0 = _____

You also should begin to learn your 8 times table. Here are the facts:

0 × 8 = 0	5 × 8 = 40	10 × 8 = 80
1 × 8 = 8	6 × 8 = 48	11 × 8 = 88
2 × 8 = 16	7 × 8 = 56	12 × 8 = 96
3 × 8 = 24	8 × 8 = 64	
4 × 8 = 32	9 × 8 = 72	

Have a go

Now make a list of all the answers you coloured red in question 1 and write the correct answers. These are facts that you must work harder to learn. Try saying the questions and answers aloud in silly voices.

Teacher's tips

Remember that multiplication can be done in any order, so once you know 8 × 3 = 24 you already know that 3 × 8 = 24! You probably already know a lot of your 7, 8, and 9 times tables.

9: Multiplication

Once you know your times tables you can begin to multiply larger numbers.

To do this it can help to be able to **partition** a number.

Partitioning a number means splitting it into parts, like this.

17 = 10 + 7   **32 = 30 + 2**

Here the numbers have been partitioned into tens and units.

Now when multiplying, each part can be multiplied separately and added together at the end.

17 × 3	=	10 × 3	+	7 × 3	
	=	30	+	21	= 51

32 × 4	=	30 × 4	+	2 × 4	
	=	120	+	8	= 128

Get ready

Answer each question using partitioning.

1 14 × 3 _____

_____

2 15 × 4 _____

_____

3 23 × 4 _____

_____

4 31 × 5 _____

_____

Let's practise

Answer each question using partitioning.

5 45 × 3 _____

6 34 × 4 _____

7 62 × 5 _____

Use a similar method to solve these problems.

8 How much does it cost to buy three plants, each costing £14?

_____

9 Each side of a square measures 34 mm. What is the perimeter of the square (the distance all the way around the edge)?

_____

Have a go

Choose three of these digits to make a multiplication question.

☐☐ × ☐ =

How many different questions and answers can you make?

Teacher's tips

Make this method easier by choosing to think about each multiplication problem in the way you find easiest – remember they can be solved either way round! The key thing is to take your time, doing one step at a time.

We use fractions to help us describe when something has been split into parts that are smaller than one whole.

This pizza has been split into 8 equal pieces.

Each piece is called one eighth which is written $\frac{1}{8}$.

The number on the bottom of the fraction shows how many equal pieces the whole has been split into.

Write a fraction to show what each piece of the whole pizza would be called.

1

3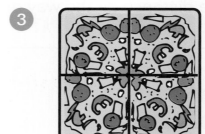

_____

2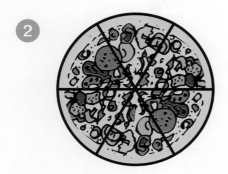

4

_____

_____

Join each shape with a fraction to show the part shaded.

5

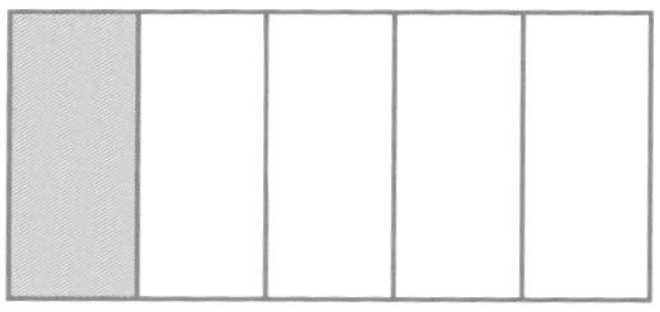

6

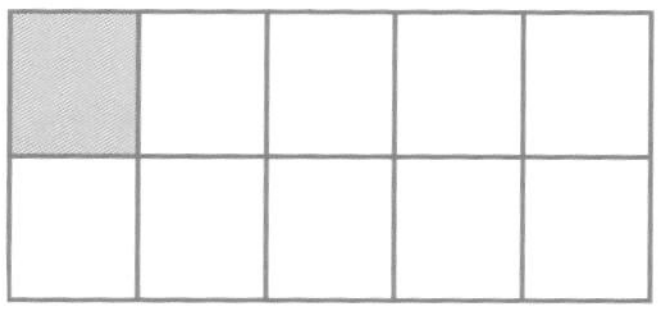

7

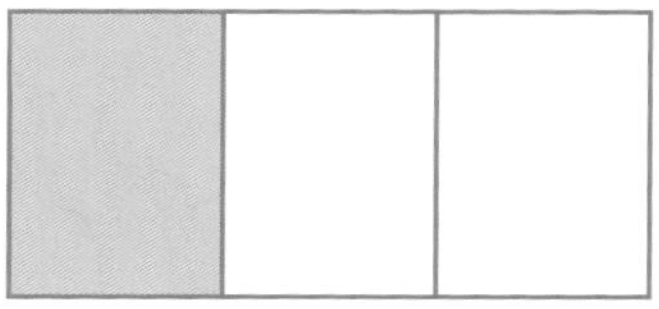

8

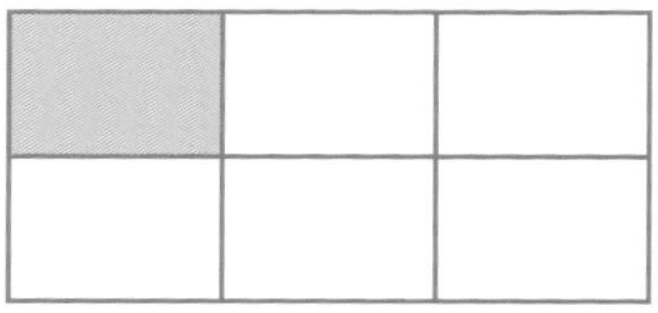

9

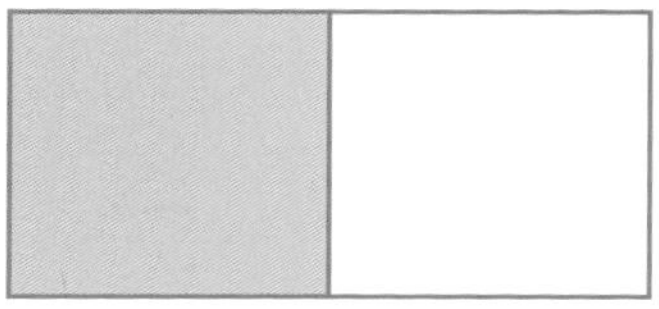

$\dfrac{1}{6}$

$\dfrac{1}{2}$

$\dfrac{1}{8}$

$\dfrac{1}{10}$

$\dfrac{1}{5}$

$\dfrac{1}{3}$

$\dfrac{1}{4}$

10   Now write all the fractions above in order of size, starting with the smallest.

_____

_____

Have a go

Think of as many places as you can in real life where you use fractions to describe things, such as 'half time', 'quarter past', 'half price', etc. Make a list.

Teacher's tips

The number at the bottom of a fraction (the denominator) shows how many parts something has been split into in total; the number at the top (the numerator) shows how many of those parts we're talking about.

11: Fractions

The fractions you have been looking at all had the number 1 on top, like $\frac{1}{8}$, $\frac{1}{3}$ or $\frac{1}{10}$. We call these unit fractions.

Sometimes we need to describe more than one part of a whole. For this we need to use different numbers on top!

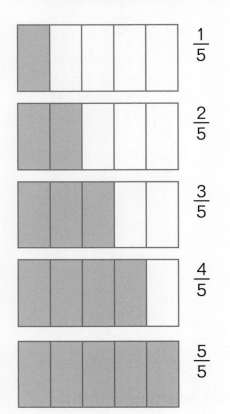

Notice that when the number on the top (the numerator) and the number on the bottom (the denominator) are the same, the fraction is equivalent to one whole.

Get ready

1. Write what fraction of each shape is shaded.

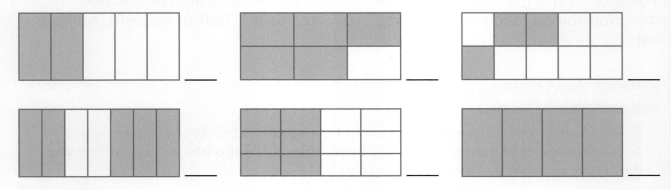

Let's practise

2 Ring the fractions that are equivalent to one whole.

$\frac{1}{10}$ $\frac{3}{4}$ $\frac{4}{4}$ $\frac{1}{2}$ $\frac{3}{3}$ $\frac{5}{6}$

$\frac{1}{4}$ $\frac{4}{5}$

$\frac{2}{2}$ $\frac{7}{8}$ $\frac{4}{8}$

$\frac{9}{10}$ $\frac{3}{5}$ $\frac{1}{4}$ $\frac{7}{7}$

$\frac{2}{4}$ $\frac{8}{8}$

Fill in the missing numbers. One has been done for you.

3 $\frac{1}{4} + \frac{\boxed{3}}{4} = 1$

5 $\frac{4}{5} + \frac{\boxed{}}{5} = 1$

4 $\frac{5}{8} + \frac{\boxed{}}{8} = 1$

6 $\frac{3}{10} + \frac{\boxed{}}{10} = 1$

Have a go

Write as many pairs of fractions as you can that have a total of 1.

117

12: Tenths

When you split or divide something into 10 equal parts these are called tenths.

One tenth is shown by the fraction $\frac{1}{10}$.

We can find one tenth of a shape, quantity or number by dividing by 10.

$\frac{1}{10}$ of 40 means that 40 is split into 10 equal parts.

4	4	4	4	4
4	4	4	4	4

So $\frac{1}{10}$ of 40 = 4

Get ready

Write what fraction of each shape is shaded.

 1

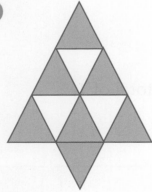

_____

3

_____

2

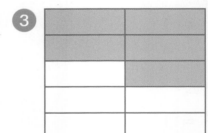

_____

4

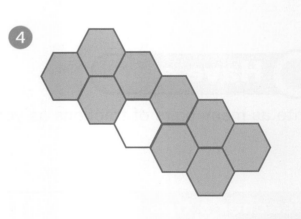

_____

Let's practise

Find one tenth by dividing by 10.

5 $\dfrac{1}{10}$ of 50 = _____

6 $\dfrac{1}{10}$ of 90 = _____

7 One tenth of 120 = _____

8 One tenth of 30 = _____

9 One tenth of 250 = _____

10 Count on in tenths to continue this sequence.

$\dfrac{1}{10}, \dfrac{2}{10}, \dfrac{3}{10}, \underline{}, \dfrac{5}{10}, \dfrac{6}{10}, \underline{}, \dfrac{8}{10}, \underline{}, \underline{}$

11 Count back in tenths to continue this sequence:

$\dfrac{13}{10}, \dfrac{12}{10}, \dfrac{11}{10}, \underline{}, \dfrac{9}{10}, \dfrac{8}{10}, \underline{}, \dfrac{6}{10}, \underline{}, \underline{}, \underline{}, \underline{}$

12 Is this statement true or false?

If three whole pizzas are shared equally between 10 people, each person will get $\dfrac{3}{10}$ of a pizza. _____

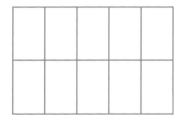 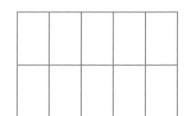 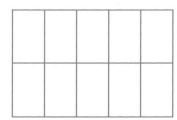

Have a go

Look on the internet. Find out how one tenth is written as a decimal.

Teacher's tips

Tenths are a really important fraction because they link easily to our decimal system of writing numbers and measuring mass, volume and length (using metric units). We also have 10 fingers so that helps calculate some fractions!

13: 2D shape

How well do you know the names and properties of two-dimensional (2D) shapes? These are shapes that can be drawn on paper and have no depth.

The most common 2D shapes have sides that are straight or curved. Those with straight sides have an angle at each corner (vertex).

Get ready

Name each shape.

1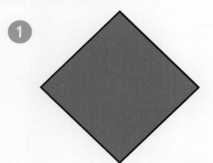
_____

2
_____

3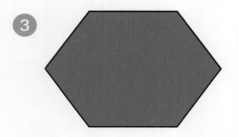
_____

4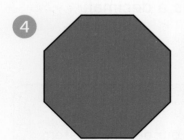
_____

5
_____

6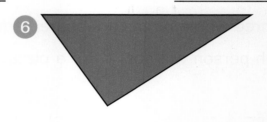
_____

7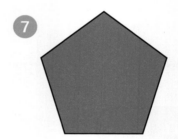
_____

8
_____

Let's practise

When a 2D shape has only straight sides it is called a polygon.

9 Which of the shapes opposite are polygons?

_____

10 Which of the polygons opposite has at least one right-angle?

_____

11 Tick to show whether each shape opposite is symmetrical.

You will need a ruler for these questions.

12 Draw a quadrilateral that has at least one right angle.

13 Draw an octagon that has no right angles.

Have a go

Look around your house or school. Try to find different shapes, such as windows that are rectangles, wallpaper that has hexagons, wrapping paper with circles, duvet covers with triangles, etc. Make a list of the shapes you find.

Teacher's tips

We normally think of shapes in their regular form (when all sides are the same length), but they can also be 'irregular'. Count the number of sides carefully to know what category the shape is in, you may be surprised!

14: 3D shape

How well do you know the names and properties of three-dimensional (3D) shapes? These are shapes that have length, width and height (or depth). You can hold them in your hand.

The most common 3D shapes have faces that are flat or curved, edges that are straight or curved. Those with straight edges have angles at each corner (vertex).

Get ready

Name each shape.

1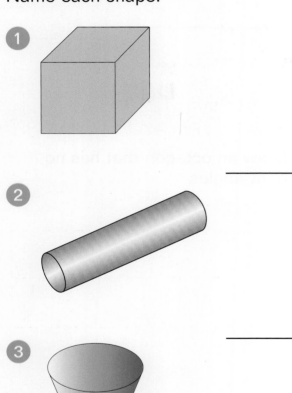

_____

2

_____

3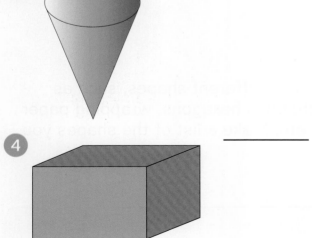

_____

4

_____

5

_____

6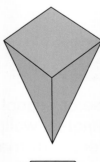

_____

7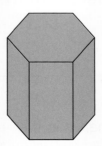

_____

8

_____

Let's practise

When a 3D shape has only straight edges it is called a polyhedron.

9 Which of the shapes opposite are polyhedrons?

_____

10 How many faces does a square-based pyramid have? _____

11 How many edges does a triangular prism have? _____

12 How many vertices (corners) does a cone have? _____

13 Fill in this table to show the number of faces, vertices and edges.

Shape	Number of faces	Number of vertices	Number of edges
Cube	6		
Triangular prism			
Cuboid			
Square-based pyramid			

Have a go

Look around your house or school. Try to find different shapes, such as chocolate boxes that are prisms or cuboids, tubes of sweets that are cylinders, balls that are spheres, etc. Make a list of the shapes you find.

Teacher's tips

A common category of 3D shape is a prism: these are shapes with identical parallel bases and they always take their name from the shape of the base (e.g. a triangular prism).

15: Angles

An angle is an amount of turn and is measured in degrees. There are 360 degrees in a full turn, 180 degrees in a half turn and 90 degrees in a quarter turn.

We show degrees using the symbol °, like this.

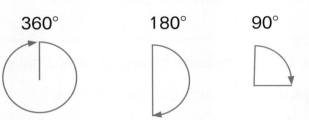

Right angles (quarter turns) are often found in shapes, like this.

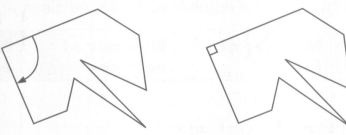

We mark them like this.

Get ready

1 Mark all the angles that are right angles.

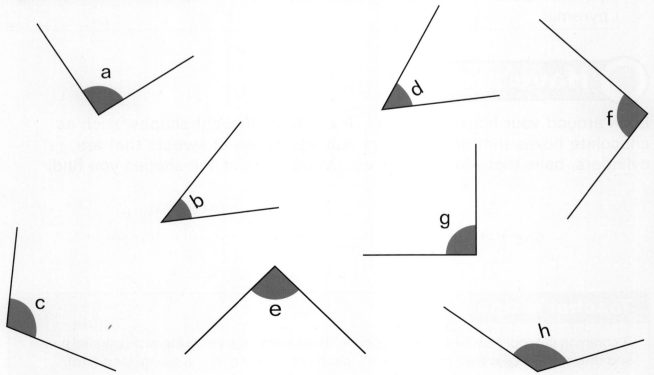

Let's practise

2 Mark any right angles in these shapes.

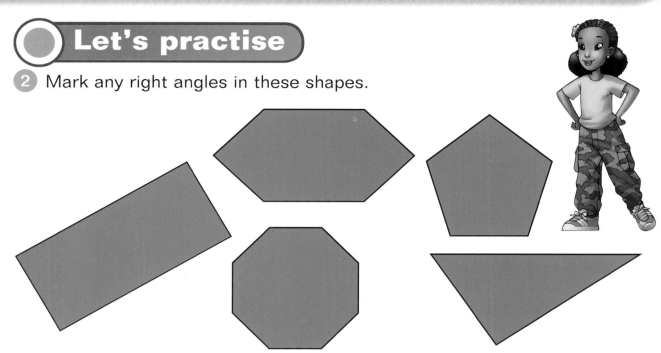

Angles less than a right angle are called **acute angles**. Angles larger than a right angle but less than two right angles are **obtuse angles**.

3 Write acute or obtuse for each angle below.

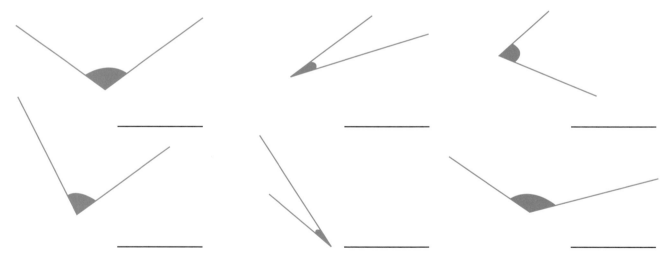

Have a go

Look on the internet to find out why a triangle is called a triangle.

Teacher's tips

Whatever position a shape is in, the angle is always the amount of 'turn' from one line to the other. You might find it helps to turn the paper so that one line points upwards (12 on a clock).

16: Measures

Make sure you know how to write these units of measurement and their abbreviations:

For length:
millimetres (mm), centimetres (cm), metres (m)

For mass:
grams (g), kilograms (kg)

For capacity:
millilitres (ml) and litres (l)

 **Get ready**

Write the most likely unit for each measurement. One has been done for you.

1. The capacity of a bath is 200 _____litres_____.

2. The length of a my fingernail is 7 _____.

3. The width of a CD is 12 _____.

4. The mass of a washing machine is 80 _____.

5. The height of a door is 200 _____.

6. The capacity of a kettle is 2 _____.

7. The mass of a mobile phone is 150 _____.

8. The capacity of a mug is 300 _____.

Let's practise

9   Use a ruler to measure and label the length of each side
     of this rectangle in centimetres.

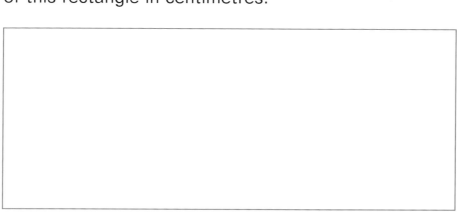

_____

10   Now add up the lengths to give the perimeter of the rectangle.

_____

11   Measure the sides and give the perimeter of this triangle.

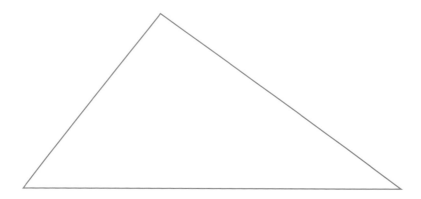

Have a go

Use a measuring jug and water to investigate the capacity of different cups
and mugs in your house.

Teacher's tips

Check the scale on the ruler that you're using – many have centimetres, millimetres
and inches – and make sure to carefully position the zero at one end of the line being
measured. Note the length of each line by the picture.

17: Telling the time

We show times on digital and analogue clocks.
Digital clocks use three or four digits to show the time.
Analogue clocks use hands and a clock-face.

These clocks show the same time.

Twenty-five to eleven   Ten thirty-five

Write each time in words. Include the words 'past' or 'to' in your answers.

1

_____

3

_____

2

_____

4

_____

Let's practise

Draw hands on the clocks to show the given time.

5 Half past seven   **6** Ten to eight   **7** Quarter past three

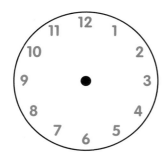   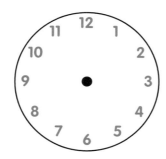   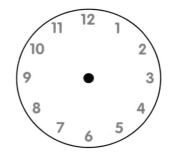

8 Twenty-five minutes past one   **9** Seventeen minutes to six

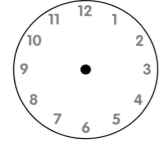   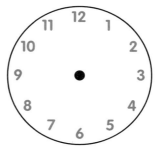

10 Write each time above in digital form. One has been done for you.

_____7:30_____   _____   _____

_____   _____

 Have a go

Use a TV guide to see what time some of your favourite programmes start.
Write each time in digital form and in words. Then draw a clock-face with
hands to show them.

Teacher's tips

When using digital clocks remember that there are only 60 minutes in an hour, so
although they look like decimal numbers they work very differently. After :59 you
start a new hour and the minutes are written :00.

18: Time

When measuring time we can use any of the following units of measurements.

seconds, minutes, hours, days, weeks, months, years, decades, centuries...

Make sure you know how many of days are in each month of the year. You can learn this rhyme to help you:

Thirty days has September, April, June and November,
All the rest have thirty-one
Except for February alone,
which has twenty-eight most of the time,
but in leap year twenty-nine.

Get ready

Write the number of days in each month.

1. January _____

2. November _____

3. July _____

4. August _____

5. June _____

6. October _____

7. April _____

8. March _____

9. September _____

10. May _____

11. December _____

12. February _____ or _____

Let's practise

How many days are there in these months?

13 March and April together? _____

14 January and June together? _____

15 July and August together? _____

16 May and October together? _____

17 September and June together? _____

18 October, November and December together?

_____

Which is longer?

19 2 months or 70 days? _____

20 3 months or 80 days? _____

21 90 seconds or 1 minute? _____

22 100 seconds or 2 minutes? _____

23 250 seconds or 5 minutes? _____

Have a go

Look on the internet. Find out another way to learn the number of days in each month, using your knuckles.

Teacher's tips

Start by learning the number of seconds in a minute, minutes in an hour, and hours in a full day. Get a clock at home and keep practising by quizzing friends and family about the time!

19: Data handling

When solving problems involving bar charts and pictograms, be careful to read the scale or key.

 **Get ready**

A shop sells DVDs of films. The DVDs are in different sections according to the type of film.

This pictogram shows the number of DVDs sold from each section on Saturday.

		Key ◎ = 10 DVDs
Horror	◎ ◎ ◎ ◎	
Drama	◎ ◎ ◎ ◎ ◎ ◎ ◎ ◎	
Children's	◎ ◎ ◎	
Comedy	◎ ◎ ◎ ◎ ◎	

Look at this pictogram.

How many packs of DVDs of each type were sold?

1 Horror _____

2 Drama _____

3 Children's _____

4 Comedy _____

5 How many more Drama DVDs were sold than Horror DVDs? _____

6 How many fewer Children's DVDs were sold than Comedy DVDs?

_____

Let's practise

7 Now draw a bar chart of the same information shown in the pictogram. It has been started for you below. Remember to label the bars and axes. Use a different colour for each bar.

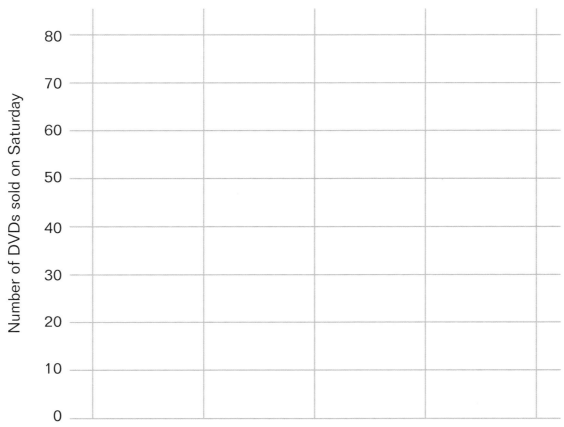

8 Make up three questions about the graph to ask someone else.

 **Have a go**

Look in a newspaper or magazine for any graphs or chart. Try to work out what they are showing.

Teacher's tips

The most common mistake made when reading diagrams is to rush and not read the labels, scales or key carefully. Take your time, graphs can look similar but give very different information!

How have I done?

1. Partition this number. 436   ____ ____ ____

2. Order these numbers, smallest first.

   263, 265, 189, 273, _____ , _____ , _____ , _____

3. Continue this sequence by counting on in 100s.

   309, 409, 509, 609, _____ , _____ , _____

4. Count in steps of 8.

   _8_ ___ ___ ___ ___ ___ ___ ___ ___ ___ ___ ___

5. Complete the addition and subtraction grids below.

+	8	4	7
6			
9			
17			

–	7	8	5
10			
13			
24			

6. Answer these questions.

   a) 386 + 100 = _____   b) 482 – 10 = _____

   c) 176 + 10 = _____   d) 503 – 100 = _____

7. Do these calculations.

```
   6 2 4            6 7 1
 + 1 5 3          – 1 2 3
 _____          _____

 _____          _____
```

```
    2 8 5              8 4 5
  + 4 7 8            − 1 8 9
  ─────────          ─────────

  ─────────          ─────────
```

8 Do these multiplications.

$6 \times 4 =$ _____ $12 \times 5 =$ _____ $10 \times 8 =$ _____

$15 \times 5 =$ _____

_____

$23 \times 4 =$ _____

_____

9 Write what fraction of each shape is shaded.

   _____   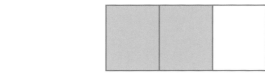   _____

10 Fill in the missing numbers in this sequence.

$\dfrac{1}{10}$, ─── , $\dfrac{3}{10}$, ─── , $\dfrac{5}{10}$, ─── , ─── , $\dfrac{8}{10}$, ─── , 1 whole

11 Write the most likely unit for each measurement.

The width of my hand is 10 _____.

The height of a door is 2 _____.

12 A digital clock shows 3:50.

Draw hands on this clock to match this time.

13 How many days are there in June and July together? _____

Problem Solving

- Fun exercises to work through
- Master problem solving skills

Place value questions may ask you to estimate a total, or 'round' a number to 10 or 100. You will also need to know the value of the digits within a number.

Charlie said it's really important we 'know our place'! He set us some questions to help us understand.

Get ready

1. Abbie drove a round trip of 287 miles to visit her Granny. How many miles is that, rounded to the nearest 100? _____

2. Charlie cycled 91 miles on a sponsored cycle ride. How many miles is that, rounded to the nearest 100? _____

3. If Abbie had driven 300 miles further on her visit, how many miles would that have been exactly? _____

4. If Charlie had cycled 20 miles less on his sponsored ride, how many miles would that have been exactly? _____

Abbie said she 'values' us so much she set us these questions.

5 If Megan takes 334 from 1250, will the answer be closer to 1300, 900 or 1000?

_____

6 A pilot flies 689 km on Saturday and 816 km on Sunday. Is the total distance flown closer to 1000 km, 1500 km or 2000 km?

_____

7 Write the number in words which is 5000 less than sixty-three thousand four hundred and thirty-six.

_____

8 Kim has the digit cards 5, 2, 7 and 9. What is the highest 3-digit number he can make? Write your answer in words.

_____

9 Amina has the digit cards 6, 7, 3, 9 and 8. What is the second smallest 4-digit number she can make? _____

Have a go

Write down the exact date of your birthday in numbers.

For example, 24 December 1999 would be 24/12/1999.

Now write that in words: twenty-fourth/twelfth/one thousand nine hundred and ninety-nine.

Teacher's tips

When making the highest number from a set of digits it's their place value that's important; you'll want as many thousands as possible, then as many hundreds, tens and units. For the smallest number the opposite is true.

2: Fractions

Charlie and Abbie took us for a trip to the seaside. It was one of the best days out ever!

When we came back to Kids Club, we did some problems about fractions. We had to find a fraction of a total, and work out what fraction a smaller number is of a bigger number.

Get ready

1. I found 16 shells by a rock pool. Abbie told me that one quarter of them were clam shells. How many of my shells were clam shells? _____

2. I made a sandcastle with 10 towers. However, when Alfie was playing cricket, he ran to catch the ball and squashed two of the towers! What fraction of my towers were left? _____

3. How many more towers would Alfie need to squash to ruin half of my sandcastle towers? _____

4. Megan wrote her name in the sand using 100 pebbles. Kim did the same using a quarter of that amount. How many pebbles did Kim use to write his name? _____

Let's practise

Here's what happened in the afternoon.

5 We beachcombed along $\frac{1}{2}$ a kilometre of the beach and found all sorts of things. How far did we go in metres? _____

6 Charlie found 30 different shells. He kept one fifth of them to use for artwork at Kids Club. How many shells did Charlie bring back?

_____

7 Abbie had a £5 note and bought us five children an ice cream for £1 each. What fraction of £5 is £1? _____

8 There were 12 swimmers in the sea. A quarter of them had body-boards, and a third had inflatable toys. How many swimmers did not have an inflatable or a body-board? _____

9 Kim flew a kite for $\frac{2}{5}$ths of an hour. Jamelia flew her kite for $\frac{3}{10}$ths of an hour. Who flew their kite for longer, Kim or Jamelia?

_____

Have a go

These equivalent fractions can really help you with fraction problems. Learn them!

$\frac{1}{2} = \frac{2}{4} = \frac{3}{6} = \frac{4}{8} = \frac{5}{10}$

$\frac{1}{3} = \frac{2}{6} = \frac{3}{9} = \frac{4}{12} = \frac{5}{15}$

$\frac{1}{4} = \frac{2}{8} = \frac{3}{12} = \frac{4}{16} = \frac{5}{20}$

$\frac{1}{5} = \frac{2}{10} = \frac{3}{15} = \frac{4}{20} = \frac{5}{25}$

Teacher's tips

Think of the line in a proper fraction as meaning 'out of every', so $\frac{1}{5}$ of 20 means '1 out of every 5' in 20. There are 4 5s in 20, so $\frac{1}{5}$ of 20 = 4.

3: Decimals

We needed to decorate the hall at Kids Club for a special ceremony – Kids Club had won an award from the council for being the best run after-school club in the area. We decided to make all our own decorations and impress the mayor even more!

We had to solve a lot of problems with decimals, to do with money or measures. Remember, decimal numbers are not whole numbers. For example, the decimal 6.8 is in between 6 and 7.

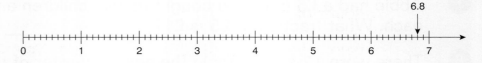

Get ready

1. Abbie spent £6.85 on sugar paper so we could make streamers. This was half the amount of money Abbie had to spend on paper in total. How much money did Abbie have to spend on paper?

   _____

2. Alfie had 1.5 m of string to tie up some balloons. He cut off 85 cm. How long was the remaining piece of string? _____

3. Jamelia made six streamers each 2.4 m long. How long were the streamers altogether? _____

4. Abbie bought 18 rolls of ribbon and spent £4.50. How much was one roll of ribbon? _____

Let's practise

The mayor came and presented us with a certificate and prize. We were all very proud!

5 Megan made a big banner to welcome the mayor. It was rectangular and measured 125 cm along the top and 250 cm down the side. What was the total length in metres of the perimeter (distance around) of the banner?

_____

6 Kim cut five lengths of ribbon each measuring 2.7 m. What was the total amount of ribbon Kim cut in metres? _____

7 Drinks were served when the mayor arrived. The children drank 7.3 litres of juice; the mayor drank 500 ml of mineral water. What was the difference in litres? _____

8 There were 6.3 kg of snacks and nibbles for the guests. However, the mayor's speech went on for ages so only 2.9 kg were eaten! How many kilograms of snacks and nibbles were left? _____

9 The mayor awarded Kids Club £500 to be spent on improving the outdoor area. £50.75 was spent on plants, £75.95 on gardening tools and £140.50 on new seating. How much was left to spend in the future? _____

Have a go

Make a set of digit cards 1 to 9. Shuffle them and choose four. Work methodically to make as many decimal numbers that have two digits after the decimal point as you can. Then place the numbers in order, smallest first.

Teacher's tips

Convert all the units to be the same before you try to calculate the answer, then at the end express the answer using the most appropriate units (so 1.1 m is better than 1100 mm).

4: Addition and subtraction

All the children began collecting wildlife stickers and putting them in an album. We swap any spares – I've nearly completed the collection!

We found we had to solve problems in lots of different measures. Remember to mark the correct units – litres, metres or stickers.

Get ready

1. There are 100 stickers in the collection. I have 84. How many more do I need to make a hundred? _____

2. Megan has 10 fewer stickers than Jamelia, who has 55. How many stickers does Megan have? _____

3. Jamelia is given 26 spare stickers by Kim. How many does she have now? _____

4. I dropped 35 of my 78 spares into a puddle! How many spares do I have left? _____

Let's practise

Once we completed our wildlife collection we started another one on Super Cars. There were more stickers to collect so it took a bit longer.

5 Amina has 53 super-car stickers. Kim has 68 more. How many super-car stickers does Kim have? _____

6 Jamelia got bored with super cars and swapped 45 of her 72 stickers for a music magazine. How many stickers did she have left? _____

7 I had 274 super-car stickers in my album and 128 spares. How many super-car stickers did I have in total? _____

8 Between us all we had 607 wildlife stickers. That is 244 fewer than the total amount of super-car stickers we had between us. How many super-car stickers did we have in total? _____

9 One page of the super-car sticker album holds 25 stickers. Megan has completed three pages so far. There are 500 stickers needed to complete the collection. How many more pages does she need to fill?
_____

Have a go

Use three numbers and the + and − signs to make different number sentences that total

a) 20 _____

b) 100 _____

Teacher's tips

Go through the question underlining the *values* and the *actions*, and writing them in numbers and maths symbols above. This will help you make a number sentence for what the question is asking, and make it easier to solve.

We had a table-top sale to raise money to buy some seeds and fertiliser for the Kids Club vegetable garden. We all brought in our old toys and books and sold them to the mums, dads, child-minders and children after school.

We found that money problems can be adding, subtracting, multiplying or dividing. They often ask you to work out how much change you need after paying for something.

Get ready

1. I sold my Action Men for 60p each. I sold three Action Men in total. How much did I make by selling all three Action Men? _____

2. Jamelia sold Pretty Poppy Pocket Dolls for 50p each. She made £4.50 from selling the dolls. How many did she sell? _____

3. Megan's younger brother brought some coins to spend. He had a 50p coin, three 20p coins and four 10p coins. How much did he have in total? _____

4. Amina made £10. She raised £3.75 selling books, £1.89 selling board games and the rest from selling plastic jewellery. How much did Amina raise by selling jewellery? _____

Let's practise

Here are some of the toys that we had for sale.

5 What is the total cost of the most expensive and the least expensive of the items? _____

6 I sold two bikes. How much did I raise selling the bikes?

_____

7 Jamelia's little sister had £5. She wanted to spend as much of this as possible. Which two items could she buy and how much change would she get? _____

8 One of the dads bought six footballs for the after-school football club. How much did he spend? _____

9 How much was raised by selling 2 bikes, 8 footballs, 3 computer games, 1 car, 4 boats and 2 trains? _____

Have a go

Imagine you have £20 to spend for your birthday. Look through a toy catalogue and choose three different items to spend your money on. Try and spend as close to £20 as you can.

Teacher's tips

Make notes on a piece of paper with all the important parts of the question to help you order your thinking and calculations.

6: Time

In the school holidays we run a 'Kids Camp' where the children can come and do all sorts of activities. We have lots of time to have fun!

Time questions have a start and finish time. You will usually have to work out how long it is in between.

Get ready

1. On Monday mornings, we do roller-skating in the gym from 9.30 a.m. until 10.15 a.m. How many minutes is that? _____

2. On Tuesday mornings, Abbie does a bicycle repairs workshop. This lasts from 9.45 a.m. until 11.00 a.m. The children learn how to fix their bikes! How long does the workshop last in minutes? _____

3. On Wednesday mornings, there is an indoor hockey tournament which lasts for $2\frac{1}{2}$ hours. It starts at 9.30 a.m. At what time does it finish? _____

4. We always break for lunch at a quarter past twelve. Lunchtime lasts for 50 minutes. What time does lunchtime end? _____

Now try these questions, which are a bit more tricky.

5 On Thursday afternoon, we do an Acting and Singing class. The class starts at 1.10 p.m. and lasts for 85 minutes. At what time does it finish?

_____

6 Friday afternoons are spent doing artwork. The children make loads of mess so we have to start clearing up early! Kids Camp finishes at 5.45 p.m. and we start clearing up 55 minutes beforehand. At what time do we begin clearing up? _____

7 We have a box of games and puzzles for when it rains. It takes Megan twice as long to complete a 100-piece jigsaw as Jamelia who takes from 9.45 a.m. to 10.30 a.m. They both start at the same time. At what time does Megan finish? _____

8 One Wednesday, the Indoor Hockey tournament overran by 25 minutes. Five matches were played. Each game should have lasted $\frac{1}{2}$ an hour. The tournament started on time at 9.30 a.m. but what time did it finish? _____

9 Kids Camp starts on Saturday 19 July and runs for exactly six weeks. On what date does it finish? _____

Have a go

Use a stop-watch to keep a 'time diary' of everything you do for a day. Write down the start and finish times of all your activities. How much time do you spend eating? How much time do you spend doing exercise? How much time do you spend asleep?

Teacher's tips

Digital time is written like decimals but is a different system. With 60 minutes in an hour it can never be more than 59 minutes past, as 1 minute later moves to the next o'clock. Add minutes up in groups of 60 to make hours.

7: Measures – length

Charlie and I took the children on a country walk. They measured and recorded some of the things they found in the countryside and generally had a good time!

Problems about length can be about very short lengths like millimetres and centimetres or long lengths like kilometres or miles. The problems may be about a journey or measuring an object.

Get ready

1. Kim found a big leaf. It was 26 cm long. Alfie found an even bigger leaf – it was 9 cm longer. How long was Alfie's leaf? _____

2. Charlie made a bow from a yew tree branch. He then made four arrows by cutting a straight, thin stick into equal lengths. Each arrow was 40 cm long and tipped with a cork to make it safe. How long was the stick before Charlie cut it? _____

3. Charlie fired two arrows in a field. The first one landed 80 m ahead; the second landed 25 m further away! How far did the second arrow travel? _____

4. Jamelia had a go. She pulled the bow-string back as far as it would go and fired! The arrow went out of sight. When she found it, it had gone 150 cm further than Charlie's second arrow. How far did Jamelia shoot her arrow? _____

Let's practise

The children had an eventful afternoon . . .

5 Amina caught a frog with her net. It was 92 mm long. Megan caught one which was 28 mm longer. How long was Megan's frog? _____

6 I found a badger set with four tunnels but no badgers. The holes were 65 cm, 72 cm, 58 cm and 77 cm wide. What was the total width of all the holes? _____

7 Kim jumped 1.9 m over a stream. Jamelia jumped over the stream where it measured 2.5 m. How much further would Kim need to have jumped to equal Jamelia? _____

8 Charlie found a ruined barn. It was quite spooky! The barn had a perimeter of 71 m and was rectangular. The length of one side was 15.5 m. What were the lengths of the other sides?

_____

9 Alfie mistook a cow for a bull! He panicked and ran across a field which was 126 m wide, jumped over a stile and ran all the way back to the mini-bus which was a further $\frac{3}{4}$ of a kilometre away! How far had Alfie run in metres? _____

Have a go

The tallest person ever was Robert Wadlow who was 272 cm tall.

How much taller than you is this?

Teacher's tips

If a problem uses different units, or some whole units and some decimal units, convert them all to be the same before you calculate the answer. Then express the answer using the most appropriate units.

8: Measures – mass

The children have been talking about their pets and Abbie and I have been telling them some amazing animal facts!

Problems about mass can be long story-type problems or short calculations. Always think about the units of measurement: grams, kilograms and tons.

Get ready

1. Amina has four gerbils which weigh 20 g, 24 g, 22 g and 26 g. What is the total weight of the four gerbils? _____

2. Jamelia has two rabbits, Warren and Wayne. They have a total weight of 1 kg. Warren weighs 450 g. How much does Wayne weigh?

    _____

3. Megan's cat Higgins is 1.6 kg heavier than Kim's kitten Alex which weighs 500 g. How heavy is Higgins? _____

4. Alfie's dog Titch eats three times a day. He has 850 g of Doggo-chunks for breakfast, 950 g of Doggo-chunks for lunch and 1.3 kg of Doggo-bix for tea. How many kilos of food does Titch eat per day?

    _____

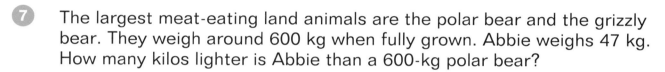

Let's practise

Here are some amazing animal facts and questions about them.

5 The world's largest rodent is the capybara which can weigh up to 79 kg. (That's heavier than me!) How much heavier is that than Amina's four gerbils (see question 1)? _____

6 The blue whale is the largest creature that has ever lived. They can grow up to 170 tons! An average car weighs 2 tons. How many times heavier is a 170-ton blue whale than an average car? _____

7 The largest meat-eating land animals are the polar bear and the grizzly bear. They weigh around 600 kg when fully grown. Abbie weighs 47 kg. How many kilos lighter is Abbie than a 600-kg polar bear?

_____

8 The tiger is the largest of the big cats and can weigh up to 280 kg. How many of Kim's kittens would you need (see question 3) to balance a 280-kg tiger? _____

9 The largest lizards in the world are dragons. The komodo dragon grows over 3 m long and weighs up to 166 kg. How much would three 166-kg komodo dragons weigh? _____

Have a go

Find out some more animal facts about weight and make up some mass problems for your friends to solve.

Teacher's tips

There are 1000 grams in a kilogram, which can be confusing as there are only 100 centimetres in a metre – don't get caught out!

9: Measures – capacity

It is a really hot day today. We have filled the Kids Club paddling pool with 70 litres of cool water and are having a great time!

Capacity problems are all about how much containers can hold. You might need to find out the difference between two capacities.

Get ready

1. A water balloon holds 500 ml of water. Alfie throws two full water balloons at Charlie! How much water is that in total? _____

2. There are 69 litres left in the pool. Charlie fills up his giant water pistol with 4 litres of water. How much is left in the pool? _____

3. Charlie thought Abbie had thrown the balloons! He squirts 800 ml of the 4 litres at Abbie – she's drenched. How much water is left in Charlie's water pistol? _____

4. Abbie gets her own back by throwing three water balloons each containing 400 ml of water. Bulls-eye. All of them hit! How much water do the balloons hit Charlie with? _____

The pool now contains 63.8 litres of water – but for how much longer?

5 Alfie tries to soak Abbie next. He pours 8.9 litres from the pool into a bucket and aims it at Abbie. How much is left in the pool now? _____

6 He misses and hits me! Not funny. Abbie fills three water balloons with 350 ml of water and I fill two balloons with 400 ml. Alfie doesn't stand a chance! How much water did we throw at Alfie? _____

7 Time to clear up and dry off. Abbie fills a 7-litre bucket five times and waters the vegetable patch. How much water goes on the vegetable patch? _____

8 Charlie says everyone can have a chocolate milk-shake! He needs 250 ml of milk for a milk-shake and has two 1.5-litre bottles of milk. How many milk-shakes can Charlie make? _____

9 Five people don't want a milk-shake and would prefer a fruit punch. Abbie has a recipe for three people. How much of each ingredient would she need for five people?

_____

_____

Fruit Punch (for 3 people)

1.5 l lemonade

210 ml fruit juice

75 ml lemon juice

Have a go

Using a measuring jug and water, investigate the capacities of different cups and mugs in your house. Which ones could hold a whole can of cola (330 ml) without any spillage?

Teacher's tips

There are 1000 millilitres in a litre – so 1.2 litres is 1200 millilitres (not 120 as sometimes people write). Remember 'milli' means 'one thousandth of a'.

These are some puzzles Charlie and Abbie set for us when it was raining one afternoon. See how you get on!

Number puzzles might ask you to look for patterns or they might ask you to experiment with different numbers to see if they fit. If one way doesn't work then try something else.

Get ready

1. When I add 19 to my number I get 45. What is my number?
_____

2. When I add 10 to my number and then halve the answer I get 11. What is my number? _____

3. When I divide my number by 4, then add 12, I get 21. What is my number? _____

4. When I multiply my number by 8 and then subtract 15, I get 41. What is my number? _____

Let's practise

These are a bit harder. Think clearly and take it step by step.

5 I am a square number less than 100.
The sum of my digits is 10.
What am I? _____

6 I am the sum of the factors of 32.
What am I? _____

7 We are multiples of 3. We are more than 10
but less than 50. We are also multiples of 4.
What are we? _____

8 The total of two numbers is 36. One number is twice the value of
the other. What are the two numbers?

_____

9 Which two mathematical symbols $(+ - \times \div)$ must you put into this
sum to give the answer 57?

76 ? 15 ? 20 = 57 _____

Have a go

Use these words to make up three number puzzles for a friend.

> **More than, sum, difference,
> product, factor, multiple,
> less than, square, total**

Teacher's tips

Write the problem as a number sentence with a '?' where the missing information is.
Remember equals means 'is the same as'. Experiment swopping '?' with different
numbers until you get the answer.

Problems involving patterns and sequences often ask you to work out the differences between the numbers. Practise counting on or back from any number in steps of any single-digit number. Then try counting on or back in steps of any two-digit number. Practice makes perfect!

Get ready

1. Write the next three numbers in this sequence and then write the rule in words. 23, 20, 17, 14, _____

2. Write the next three numbers in this sequence.
   21, 28, 35, 42, _____, _____, _____
   What would be the fifth number after forty-two? _____

3. Complete this sequence then write the rule in words.
   _____, _____, 13, 18, _____, 28, _____

   _____

4. Complete this sequence then write the rule in words. 7, 18, 29, 40,
   _____, _____

   _____

I've put these number patterns into a challenge for you to try.
Can you get them all correct and save the world?!

5 Your spaceship is under attack from Aliens! You need to press the right buttons on your spaceship computer to raise a shield and deflect their laser. Which three buttons must you press next?
46, 39, 32, 25, _____, _____, _____

6 The Aliens have fired a force beam at your home town on Earth. Deflect it by raising a giant mirror using the correct sequence of buttons or it will be destroyed!
257, 245, 233, _____, _____, _____

7 They have turned their sights back on you! Evade their laser cannons by going into hyper-space. Set your controls and go – complete the sequence. 4, 2, 0, _____, _____, _____

8 Score a direct hit by successfully firing your rockets. Ready, aim, fire!
1001, 2001, 3001, _____, _____, _____

9 Destroy the alien fleet by pressing (colouring in) the correct three buttons on the right-hand control panel. One mistake and it's all over for you and Planet Earth. Think clearly – the world depends on you!

1	2	3	4	5	6	7	8	9	10
11	12	13	14	15	16	17	18	19	20
21	22	23	24	25	26	27	28	29	30
31	32	33	34	35	36	37	38	39	40
41	42	43	44	45	46	47	48	49	50

51	52	53	54	55	56	57	58	59	60
61	62	63	64	65	66	67	68	69	70
71	72	73	74	75	76	77	78	79	80
81	82	83	84	85	86	87	88	89	90
91	92	93	94	95	96	97	98	99	100

Have a go

Patterns are not always shown in numbers. What is the missing letter in this sequence? J, F, M, A, _____, _____, J, A, S, O, N, D

Teacher's tips

To work out a number sequence, write in between the numbers what is happening each time. If it's not a number sequence work out what each letter/value represents and what is happening each time.

Kids Club have an allotment for growing fruit and vegetables. We have been planting seeds and looking after the plants.

We found there were multiplication and division problems about almost anything, even fruit and vegetables! The important thing is to know when you need to multiply or divide. Read the question carefully. What is it you are being asked to do?

Get ready

1 Jamelia has planted four rows of six strawberry plant seeds. How many seeds has she planted altogether? _____

2 Kim wants to grow some raspberries. He has planted three rows of nine bushes. How many bushes has he planted altogether?

_____

3 Alfie has 40 potato seeds to plant in five equal rows. How many potato seeds will there be in each row? _____

4 Megan has six bags of compost, Kim has six bags of compost but Charlie doesn't have any compost. Abbie shares the compost equally between the three of them. How many bags of compost do Megan, Kim and Charlie get each? _____

Let's practise

These are a bit harder; just remember to read the questions carefully.

5 Ten packets of leek seeds cost £3. Megan wants to grow some leeks but only wants two packets of seeds. How much will two packets cost? _____

6 Amina had 64 runner bean seeds. However, she left them outside and half were eaten by birds and a quarter by insects. She managed to plant the rest. How many seeds did she plant in total?

_____

7 Charlie and Abbie bought some vines to grow grapes. They bought 3 dozen for £4 each. How much did they pay for the vines?

_____

8 There are eight garden tools in a set. How many complete sets can I make from 58 tools? How many tools will be left over?

_____

9 Alfie waters his potatoes every other day. Megan waters her leeks every fifth day. They water their vegetables on the same day. When will be the next time they water their vegetables together? Work out the following three times that they will water their vegetables together. _____

Have a go

Learn your multiplication facts (and the matching division facts) up to 10 × 10. It makes Maths so much easier. You should know them all by the end of Year 4!

Teacher's tips

Look out for words in maths problems that act like signposts; 'altogether' means it's a multiplication problem and 'shared between' means it's a division problem.

13: 2D shapes

We have been cutting and making 2D shapes for a display in a classroom.

2D shape problems will often ask you questions about the properties of shapes, such as how many sides they have or whether their sides are equal in length.

Get ready

1. How many lines of symmetry does a) a square have _____ b) a rectangle have? _____

2. Which shape has an infinite (never-ending) number of lines of symmetry? _____

3. Put these polygons into this Carroll diagram.

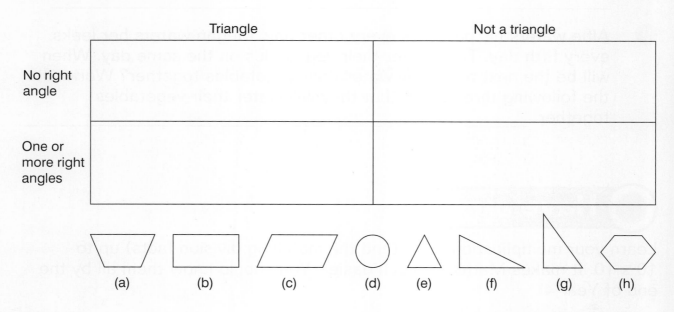

4. Draw a shape in the space here that has four sides and two right angles.

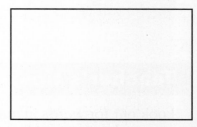

Let's practise

These are a bit harder but give them a go.
For question 9, draw a table to help you find
the answer and work methodically.

5   Charlie has a bag full of polygons. He takes out four. The sum of their sides is 14. What four shapes could they be?

_____

6   Abbie cuts a shape in half. The sum of the sides of the two new shapes is 6. What are the two new shapes? What was the original shape? _____

7   Draw a polygon that has one right angle and at least one line of symmetry.

8   Draw the reflection of this shape.

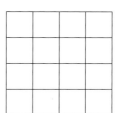

9   How many squares can you find in this grid? Look carefully! _____

Have a go

Investigate the maximum number of right angles a polygon can have.

Teacher's tips

When solving shape problems draw sketches of the shapes to help you visualise and check your ideas. Think about everyday words that might give clues to shape names; for instance an octopus has 8 legs and an octagon has 8 sides.

163

14: 3D shapes

The children have been making junk models out of 3D shapes, such as food packaging and toilet roll tubes, and asking questions about them.

Problems about 3D shapes will often ask you about their properties, such as number of faces, edges and vertices. The face is the flat bit, the edge is the long sharp bit and the vertex is the short sharp bit or corner!

Get ready

1   Megan builds a tower of eight cubes. How many faces are touching each other? _____

2   Amina chooses two different solids (3D shapes). They have 16 edges in total. Which two solids could they be?

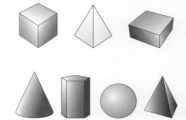

_____

3   Jamelia chooses three solids that have a total of less than 16 faces. Give two combinations of what those solids could be.

_____

_____

4   I have 5 vertices and 5 faces. Some of my faces are triangular. What am I? _____

While the children are painting their models, complete this table about solids and try the rest of the questions.

5

NAME	NUMBER OF FACES	SHAPE OF FACES	NUMBER OF EDGES	NUMBER OF VERTICES
Triangular prism				
	5	square and triangles		5
Cube				
	6	square and rectangular		
Hexagonal prism				

6 Charlie has a bag of solids. He pulls out two. They have a total of 11 faces, 20 edges and 13 vertices. What two could they be?

_____

7 He pulls out another two. They have a total of 12 faces. What two different solids could they be?

_____

8 Charlie says he is thinking of a solid. It is one he often sees on motorways when he drives his car. But it is also used to hold one of his favourite foods and at football practice. What is Charlie's solid? _____

9 This is a net of a cube. Draw the net of square-based pyramid.

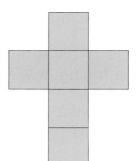

Have a go

Charlie talked about the uses of a particular solid. Look around and find examples of other 3D shapes. Why do you think they are used for different things? For example, why are bricks cuboid shaped rather than spherical?

Teacher's tips

Drawing sketches so you can label vertices, faces and edges is a great way to help with shape problems. Even better is to find objects that are common shapes and use them.

The children are going orienteering. That is a sport where you race from place to place with a map and a compass. One problem: they need to learn how to use a compass and read a simple map!

These questions can be about compass directions or finding your way around on a map or grid.

1 Jamelia is facing north. She turns clockwise through two right angles. Which direction is she facing now? _____

2 Kim is facing east. He turns anti-clockwise through three right angles. Which direction is he facing now? _____

3 Amina has turned clockwise through one right angle and is facing east. Where did she start from? _____

4 Megan is facing south-west. She has turned clockwise through one right angle and then anti-clockwise through two right angles. Where did she start? _____

Let's practise

Here is the map that the children will use for the orienteering.

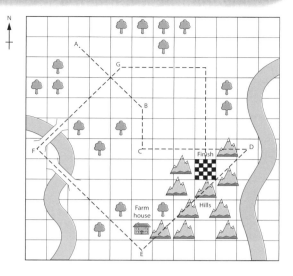

5 The children start at point A. They travel three squares south-east (SE) to square B. Describe their route from point B to point C.

_____

_____

6 The children then race to point D. What is the route they take to get there? _____

7 Describe the route from point D to point E and the type of ground they will race over. _____

8 a) When the children race from point E, as well as giving the directions to point F, describe what they see on their right.

_____

   b) What do they cross and how?

_____

9 Describe the route they take to complete the orienteering course.

_____

Have a go

Sketch a map of your garden or the park. Draw on landmarks or recognisable features.
Draw a grid over the map (at least 12 × 12). Make up your own orienteering course and write the directions for someone to complete it. (Or for a team of orienteering mice if it's your garden!)

Teacher's tips

To remember the order North, East, South, West (NESW) try this: 'Never Eat Soggy Waffles', or make up your own phrase with the letters NESW!

The children at Kids Club have done two surveys and we are going to make two suggestions to Charlie and Abbie on how to improve an already great club!

We had to read information from graphs, charts and tables.

The first survey we did was to find out the least favourite snack offered to the children at snack time.

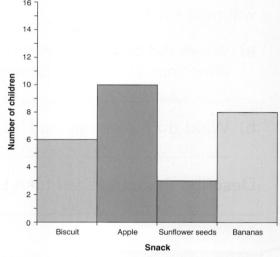

1. Which was the most popular snack?

   _____

2. How many more children preferred apples to bananas?

   _____

3. How many children were asked? _____

4. What was the answer to the question the survey was conducted for?

   _____

Let's practise

The second survey we did showed the number of lorries and vans which drove past the school at certain parts of the day.

5 When was the quietest time for lorries and vans shown by the survey?

_____

6 How many lorries and vans were counted in the second busiest period?

_____

7 What was the total number of lorries and vans counted in the two periods between 12.00 p.m. and 1.15 p.m?

_____

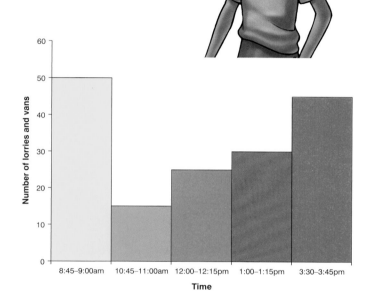

8 When were the two busiest periods for lorries and vans driving past the school? _____

9 What was the total number of lorries and vans counted in the survey?

_____

Have a go

Look at the results of the two surveys. Using the results as evidence, write two suggestions for the children for the improvement of the Kids Club.

Teacher's tips

Use a ruler to draw a feint line across to the scale when reading bar charts, and note carefully the scale being used, especially if comparing more than one chart.

17: Two-step problems

It is Abbie's birthday and we have arranged a surprise party for her. Charlie has bought all the food and we have made cards, decorations and presents. I hope Abbie likes surprises!

Two-step problems need careful thinking. It is important to work out what each step is asking you to do before you complete it.

Get ready

1. Jamelia counts 100 balloons. Half of them are red, one quarter yellow and the rest are blue. How many blue balloons are there?

   _____

2. There are six packets of six muffins and five packets of five flapjacks. How many muffins and flapjacks are there altogether?

   _____

3. There are 163 drinking straws in a box. If 30 children each take two straws, how many are left in the box? _____

4. If four bottles of sparkling fruit juice cost £2.60, how much would three bottles cost? _____

Abbie was delighted that we remembered her birthday. However, she was a bit shocked when the clown arrived which Charlie had booked!

5 Kim made 18 banana milkshakes. Each milkshake had 250 ml of milk. How many 1.5-litre cartons of milk did he use? _____

6 Which is better value, one packet of eight streamers for £1.29 or eight streamers for 17p each?

_____

_____

7 Alfie bought three candles for Abbie for £1.50 each. Megan bought her two candles for £1.25 each. How much did they spend on candles altogether? _____

8 Abbie cut her cake in 30 pieces. Each of the five children had a slice. What fraction of the cake was left? _____

9 There is a disco at the party. There are three girls dancing for every two boys. There are eight boys dancing. How many girls are dancing?

_____

Have a go

Write a two-step problem for a friend to answer. Include two different operations in the problem: addition, subtraction, multiplication or division.

Teacher's tips

Write the problem in numbers and maths symbols. Think carefully about what the question is asking – multiplication, division, addition, subtraction, fractions and so on. Solve each part on its own before putting them together to find the final answer.

How have I done?

Here's a chance to put your problem-solving skills to the test. Remember, take each problem one step at a time, read the questions carefully and check your final answer.

1. Jamelia had four digit cards 8, 4, 7 and 9. What is the second highest 3-digit number she could make? _____

2. Megan had 40 conkers. She gave eight to Kim. What fraction did she have left? _____

3. Amina spent half of her £23.60 savings on presents for her family. How much did she have left? _____

4. Alfie had 12 marbles. Kim gave him 13 more. Alfie then lost 7 in a game with Megan. How many marbles did Alfie have left? _____

5. How much change would Charlie get from a £10 note if he bought seven ice creams for 99p each? _____

6. Abbie leaves work at 6.15 p.m. After going to the supermarket, she gets home at 7.50 p.m. How long is it from when Abbie leaves work to when she gets home? _____

7. Jamelia jumped 27 cm further in the long jump competition than Amina who jumped 2.84 m. How far did Jamelia jump? _____

8. Megan's box of books weighs 4.5 kg. Kim's book bag weighs 800 g. How much heavier is Megan's box of books? _____

9. Kim drinks 2.2 litres of water per day. How many litres of water does he drink in a week? _____

10. Amina is thinking of a number. She multiplies it by 6, subtracts 4 and is left with 38. What number was Amina thinking of? _____

11. What are the missing numbers in this sequence? 12, 25, _____, 51, _____

12. Charlie cooks four packets of six sausages on the barbeque and shares them equally with eight people. How many sausages does each person get? _____

13. Abbie picks out two identical 2D shapes from a bag. The sum of the sides is 10. What are the two shapes called? _____

14. How many vertices does a triangular prism have? _____

15. Alfie is facing south-west. He takes a 90° turn clockwise and a 180° turn anticlockwise. Which compass point is he facing now?

_____

16. These are the results of a survey that Amina did to find out how children travelled to school. Cycled: 12, Walked: 25, Car: 18, Bus: 5. How many people used a form of transport to get to school?

_____

17. Charlie buys six packets of mints for 45p each and three packets of toffees for 85p each. Which costs more and by how much, the mints or the toffees? _____

18. If you get this correct it is worth **three** marks! How can you form four equilateral triangles using six matchsticks of equal length?

_____

Total marks: ___
            20

Maths tools

These may help you with some of the questions in this book.

1 WHOLE									

Fraction bar chart showing:
- $\frac{1}{2}$, $\frac{1}{2}$
- $\frac{1}{3}$, $\frac{1}{3}$, $\frac{1}{3}$
- $\frac{1}{4}$, $\frac{1}{4}$, $\frac{1}{4}$, $\frac{1}{4}$
- $\frac{1}{5}$, $\frac{1}{5}$, $\frac{1}{5}$, $\frac{1}{5}$, $\frac{1}{5}$
- $\frac{1}{6}$, $\frac{1}{6}$, $\frac{1}{6}$, $\frac{1}{6}$, $\frac{1}{6}$, $\frac{1}{6}$
- $\frac{1}{7}$, $\frac{1}{7}$, $\frac{1}{7}$, $\frac{1}{7}$, $\frac{1}{7}$, $\frac{1}{7}$, $\frac{1}{7}$
- $\frac{1}{8}$, $\frac{1}{8}$, $\frac{1}{8}$, $\frac{1}{8}$, $\frac{1}{8}$, $\frac{1}{8}$, $\frac{1}{8}$, $\frac{1}{8}$
- $\frac{1}{9}$, $\frac{1}{9}$, $\frac{1}{9}$, $\frac{1}{9}$, $\frac{1}{9}$, $\frac{1}{9}$, $\frac{1}{9}$, $\frac{1}{9}$, $\frac{1}{9}$
- $\frac{1}{10}$, $\frac{1}{10}$, $\frac{1}{10}$, $\frac{1}{10}$, $\frac{1}{10}$, $\frac{1}{10}$, $\frac{1}{10}$, $\frac{1}{10}$, $\frac{1}{10}$, $\frac{1}{10}$

Fraction, decimal and percentage equivalents

$\frac{1}{2} = 0.50 = 50\%$

$\frac{1}{4} = 0.25 = 25\%$

$\frac{3}{4} = 0.75 = 75\%$

$\frac{1}{10} = 0.10 = 10\%$

$\frac{1}{100} = 0.01 = 1\%$

$\frac{1}{3} = 0.333 = 33.33\%$

1 whole $= 1.0 = 100\%$

$\frac{1}{3} = 0.33 = 33\%$ (approximately)

$\frac{2}{3} = 0.66 = 66\%$ (approximately)

1	2	3	4	5	6	7	8	9	10
11	12	13	14	15	16	17	18	19	20
21	22	23	24	25	26	27	28	29	30
31	32	33	34	35	36	37	38	39	40
41	42	43	44	45	46	47	48	49	50
51	52	53	54	55	56	57	58	59	60
61	62	63	64	65	66	67	68	69	70
71	72	73	74	75	76	77	78	79	80
81	82	83	84	85	86	87	88	89	90
91	92	93	94	95	96	97	98	99	100

Use this hundred square to help you with your calculations.

Multiplication tables

1 x 1 = 1	2 x 1 = 2	3 x 1 = 3	4 x 1 = 4	5 x 1 = 5	6 x 1 = 6
1 x 2 = 2	2 x 2 = 4	3 x 2 = 6	4 x 2 = 8	5 x 2 = 10	6 x 2 = 12
1 x 3 = 3	2 x 3 = 6	3 x 3 = 9	4 x 3 = 12	5 x 3 = 15	6 x 3 = 18
1 x 4 = 4	2 x 4 = 8	3 x 4 = 12	4 x 4 = 16	5 x 4 = 20	6 x 4 = 24
1 x 5 = 5	2 x 5 = 10	3 x 5 = 15	4 x 5 = 20	5 x 5 = 25	6 x 5 = 30
1 x 6 = 6	2 x 6 = 12	3 x 6 = 18	4 x 6 = 24	5 x 6 = 30	6 x 6 = 36
1 x 7 = 7	2 x 7 = 14	3 x 7 = 21	4 x 7 = 28	5 x 7 = 35	6 x 7 = 42
1 x 8 = 8	2 x 8 = 16	3 x 8 = 24	4 x 8 = 32	5 x 8 = 40	6 x 8 = 48
1 x 9 = 9	2 x 9 = 18	3 x 9 = 27	4 x 9 = 36	5 x 9 = 45	6 x 9 = 54
1 x 10 = 10	2 x 10 = 20	3 x 10 = 30	4 x 10 = 40	5 x 10 = 50	6 x 10 = 60
1 x 11 = 11	2 x 11 = 22	3 x 11 = 33	4 x 11 = 44	5 x 11 = 55	6 x 11 = 66
1 x 12 = 12	2 x 12 = 24	3 x 12 = 36	4 x 12 = 48	5 x 12 = 60	6 x 12 = 72

7 x 1 = 7	8 x 1 = 8	9 x 1 = 9	10 x 1 = 10	11 x 1 = 11	12 x 1 = 12
7 x 2 = 14	8 x 2 = 16	9 x 2 = 18	10 x 2 = 20	11 x 2 = 22	12 x 2 = 24
7 x 3 = 21	8 x 3 = 24	9 x 3 = 27	10 x 3 = 30	11 x 3 = 33	12 x 3 = 36
7 x 4 = 28	8 x 4 = 32	9 x 4 = 36	10 x 4 = 40	11 x 4 = 44	12 x 4 = 48
7 x 5 = 35	8 x 5 = 40	9 x 5 = 45	10 x 5 = 50	11 x 5 = 55	12 x 5 = 60
7 x 6 = 42	8 x 6 = 48	9 x 6 = 54	10 x 6 = 60	11 x 6 = 66	12 x 6 = 72
7 x 7 = 49	8 x 7 = 56	9 x 7 = 63	10 x 7 = 70	11 x 7 = 77	12 x 7 = 84
7 x 8 = 56	8 x 8 = 64	9 x 8 = 72	10 x 8 = 80	11 x 8 = 88	12 x 8 = 96
7 x 9 = 63	8 x 9 = 72	9 x 9 = 81	10 x 9 = 90	11 x 9 = 99	12 x 9 = 108
7 x 10 = 70	8 x 10 = 80	9 x 10 = 90	10 x 10 = 100	11 x 10 = 110	12 x 10 = 120
7 x 11 = 77	8 x 11 = 88	9 x 11 = 99	10 x 11 = 110	11 x 11 = 121	12 x 11 = 132
7 x 12 = 84	8 x 12 = 96	9 x 12 = 108	10 x 12 = 120	11 x 12 = 132	12 x 12 = 144

Number line from –20 to +20

-20   -10   0   10   20

Glossary

These are words you may come across when problem solving at home or at school. Many Maths questions come in the form of 'word problems' so it's really important that you understand what you are being asked to do! Always read the question and then read it again to help your understanding. When you arrive at an answer, does it look sensible? If not, re-read the question and check your calculations.

Answer – The solution to a problem. Usually what you are trying to find out!

Calculate – To 'work out' mathematically.

Calculation – If you are asked to 'show your calculations', write down the 'working out' that you did to get your answer.

Correct – The right answer; or you can 'correct' your mistakes by changing wrong answers to right ones.

Equation – A statement that shows two mathematical expressions are equal. (Using the sign =) For example, $10 + 5 = 15$.

Jotting – Brief or short notes that you might make in your book or on paper.

Mental calculation – 'Working out' that you do in your head. When solving problems you should first try to do them in your head. If they are too hard, use a written method. If they are still too hard then use a calculator.

Method – A way of doing something. You may be asked to 'explain your method'. This means write down how you tackled the problem.

Number sentence – E.g. $46 - 32 = 14$ is a number sentence. So is $(5 \times 3) + 69 - 11 = 73$.

Operation – The four operations you need to know are addition, subtraction, multiplication and division. You may be asked 'Which operation did you use?'

Symbol – Maths uses lots of symbols. $+$, $-$, x and $\div$ are the symbols for the four operations. Others are $=$ for equals, $>$ for greater than and $<$ for less than.

Strategies for Solving Problems

At the beginning –

- How are you going to tackle the problem?
- What information do you have?
- Will you need any equipment?
- What method are you going to use?
- Can you predict or estimate the answer?

During the problem –

- Can you explain to yourself what you have done so far?
- Could there be a quicker way to do this?
- Can you see a pattern or a rule?
- Is there another method that would have worked?
- How will you show your results?

Stuck? –

- What did you do last time? What is different this time?
- Is there something you already know that might help?
- Can you put things in order?
- Would drawing a picture/graph/table/diagram help?
- Have you worked through the problem step-by-step in a logical way?

Problem solved! –

- How did you get your answer?
- Have you checked your answer?
- Does your answer make sense?
- If you were doing it again, what would you do differently?
- What have you learned or found out today?

Answers

UNIT 1

Accident: something going wrong; **Bicycle**: two-wheeled transport; **Calendar**: a list of dates; **Chocolate**: a sweet made from cocoa; **Dictionary**: a book that explains what words mean; **Experiment**: trying something out; **February**: the second month in the year; **Heart**: it pumps blood round your body; **Improve**: to get better; **Injure**: to hurt; **Island**: land surrounded by sea; **Library**: where books are kept that you can borrow; **Medicine**: liquid you drink to get better; **Nephew**: your brother's or sister's son; **Paragraph**: a chunk of text about one subject; **Quarrel**: an argument; **Quarter**: divided by four; **Sew**: to mend or decorate with thread

UNIT 2

1. It's to help them learn to count.
2. The Caribbean
3. Five verses
4. Six by six
5. Lines 1, 2 and 4

UNIT 3

1. The handwriting is to make it look like a child's diary.
2. For emphasis; to make them stand out.
3. It's a diary, and this is the first day of the week.
4. Humour; and it helps us visualise where they are.
5. USA, from 'effective today' and 'rezoned'.
6. It's non-standard English; standard English would be 'Rowley and I'.
7. stink, stank, stunk

UNIT 4

1. On the back cover of a book.
2. To persuade you to read or buy the book.
3. It's a sample from inside the book.
4. The publisher, to get you interested.
5. To show you'll find it a funny book.
6. It's a review quote, to persuade you it's funny.
7. To persuade you to read other books in the series.
8. Puffinbooks.com is the publisher; wimpykid.com is the series.

UNIT 5

1. Just the narrator and the farmer: two.
2. The wife will ask the children for help.
3. The children could ask the scarecrow, the cat and the dog.

UNIT 7

disobey: not obey; **misread**: read wrongly; **redecorate**: decorate again; **subdivide**: split into smaller pieces; **intercity**: between cities; **supermarket**: large shop; **anticlimax**: lack of climax; **autograph**: person's own signature

UNIT 8

transition, omission, electrician, inflation, confession, admission, politician, direction, confection, remission, obsession

UNIT 9
Get ready
1. I can **see** the **sea**.
2. I **would** like to chop up some **wood**.
3. I **ate eight** pieces of cake.

178

4 I asked **for four** pieces of pie.
5 I **know** there are **no** pieces left.
6 I **knew** there were no **new** pieces left.
7 There's **too** much **to** do in just **two** hours.
8 **There** is so much noise coming from that house of **theirs**.
9 **It's** all because of **its** size.
10 I can **hear** the whole sound from **here**.

Let's practise

2 That's a **fair** decision; I'll buy my **fare** on the way home.
   Adjective: fair   Noun: fare
3 We had a **great** big fire; it burned in the **grate**.
   Noun: grate   Adjective: great
4 My **heel** is hurting; I want it to **heal** soon.
   Verb: heal   Noun: heel
5 We're going to **meet** up soon; neither of us eats **meat**.
   Verb: meet   Noun: meat
6 I **missed** seeing you; it must have been because of the **mist**.
   Verb: missed   Noun: mist

UNIT 10
Let's practise

Short vowels (examples): matter, capping, copped, matting, matted, hatter, letting, betting, petting, sitting, tipping, ribbing, pipped, dinner, cropped, stopped, robbed, budding, supper, tubby, cutter

Long vowels (examples): laying, staying, training, mating, hating, feeling, feeding, healing, cleaning, crying, flying, died, lied, piped, dined, moaned, groaned, rowed, robed, coped, loomed, looped, chewed, stewing, tubing, cuter

Have a go

pinning	pin/short	pining	pine/long
finned	fin/short	fined	fine/long
fussing	fuss/short	fusing	fuse/long
tapping	tap/short	taping	tape/long

UNIT 11
Get ready

1 adjective, noun, verb, noun
2 pronoun, verb, noun
3 pronoun, verb, noun, noun
4 pronoun, verb, adjective, noun

Let's practise

1 It stopped at the lights.
2 We jumped on it at the next stop.
3 It stopped at the corner.
4 We got to school late.

UNIT 12

1 We set off into the rainforest **because** we had been given a detailed map.
2 It felt very hot **although** the sun was behind clouds.
3 We were following the river **when** a snake crossed our path.
4 We wondered **if** it was poisonous.
5 We stopped **and** we trembled on the spot.
6 Then we looked in our guidebook **because** it had a list of poisonous snakes.
7 This one looked OK **so** we carried on.
8 We were pleased **when** we got back to the camp.

UNIT 13
Get ready

1 Suddenly, I dropped the jug.
2 I found the pieces on the carpet, on the floor and on the staircase.
3 The last time I did such a thing, last summer, I was so upset.

4 This time, which is even worse, it was all my own fault.
5 So I'm really sorry, Grandpa.

Let's practise
1 Alice frowned at the Mad Hatter, who was sitting opposite her.
2 The Mad Hatter nudged the dormouse, because he was asleep.
3 The tea party was ready to begin. It was half past three.
4 They ate scones and jam, and everyone loved it.
5 But who was going to clear up afterwards, as they had all gone home?

UNIT 14
Get ready
she's, she is
we'll, we will
it's, it is
wouldn't, would not
who's, who is
mustn't, must not
shouldn't, should not
shan't, shall not
won't, will not

Let's practise
2 The lady's hat
3 The child's toys
4 The men's hats
5 The ladies' cakes
6 The sheep's tails
7 The goats' milk
8 The goose's egg

UNIT 18
Get ready
MAYOR: What on earth are we going to do? Our town is overrun with rats!
1st COUNCILLOR: There are rats in the cellars!
2nd COUNCILLOR: There are rats in the streets!
PIED PIPER: Please, sirs. I think I can help you.
MAYOR: How can you do that?
PIED PIPER: I know a charm that makes animals follow me.

Let's practise
The Mayor was sitting with his Councillors, and he was very worried. "What on earth are we going to do?" he asked. "Our town is overrun with rats!"
"There are rats in the cellars!" said the First Councillor.
"There are rats in the streets!" echoed the Second Councillor.
At that point a young man came in, dressed in green and white.
"Please, sirs," he said softly. "I think I can help you."
The Mayor was amazed. "How can you do that?" he asked.
"I know a charm that makes animals follow me," said the Piper.

HOW HAVE I DONE?
Comprehension
Poetry: verses, rhyme, metre
Fiction: narrative, setting, character, plot
Playscript: cast, dialogue, stage directions
Information: factual, different sub-genres

Handwriting
diagonal, diagonal to ascender, horizontal, horizontal to ascender, up and over

Spelling
A prefix comes before a word to change its meaning.

A suffix comes at the end of a word to change its meaning.
A homophone sounds the same as another word but is spelt differently.
fatter, thinner, slimmer and taller

Grammar
adjective, noun, verb, preposition
The brown fox enjoys jumping, especially over lazy dogs.

Punctuation
The brown fox, who is quicker than the lazy dog, enjoys jumping.
The fox's bark is harsher than the dog's bark.

Composition
"Lie still," said the fox, "I'm thinking of practising my jumping."
The dog was so lazy he just yawned: "YAWN!"

WRITING AND PUNCTUATION

UNIT 1
1 Yes, for each new line
2 No
3 For each new item

UNIT 2
1 You will need:
2 What to do:

UNIT 4
dragon, noun
iceberg, noun
nutty, adjective
plumber, noun
reverse, verb

UNIT 6
1 What, Where, Who
2 Question mark
3 Only capital letter, no full stop

UNIT 8
2 Present tense

UNIT 9
1 Past tense
2 first, Early in the day, then, In the end

UNIT 10
1 Address, Date, Greeting, Message, Ending
2 Their safety
3 Asking about how the zoo is run

UNIT 12
1 Playscript (✗)
2 Speech bubbles (✗)
3 Story (✓)

UNIT 14
1 Deep, dark, black, Dank, dark, bleak, black, piercing, white, tiny, overwhelming, damp, chilling, rough

UNIT 15
Child's own answer

UNIT 16

The man woke up slowly. Where on earth was he? It was pitch black, and rather damp. At least the dog was still at his feet; that was something. But what were they doing here?

He stroked his dog's familiar fur, to stop himself trembling with panic.

"Come on, boy," he said. "We've got to get out of here."

They headed towards the source of light, stumbling through the puddles.

"If only the dog could talk," he thought. "He could remind me how we got in here."

They headed forwards, the man keeping one hand on the side of the tunnel for safety. The shape of the light got bigger and bigger, in the shape of a growing white 'n'.

At last they broke into the daylight. They were on the bank of a little canal, which snaked round the hillside to bring water to all the crops. They had been inside one of the tunnels the canal flowed through, and he must have fallen or passed out while they were in the tunnel. Never again! He would make sure he never walked through dark tunnels again for the rest of his life!

UNIT 18

Lines 2 and 4, and lines 6 and 8

UNIT 20

a   3, 7, 4
b   4, 6, 4
c   4, 8, 3

HOW HAVE I DONE?
Quiz on writing

What you need: .... Recipe / Instructions
Turn left .... Directions
Address and date .... Letter
What's your name? .... Questionnaire
PIED PIPER: .... Playscript
[*He came in slowly.*] .... Playscript
"Too right," he said .... Speech
Poem of three lines .... Haiku
He was a burly man .... Character sketch
It was a dark and stormy night .... Setting

Quiz on punctuation

1 "All right," said the clown.
2 I'll take all these: the ball, the ring and the crown.
3 The bird, which was sitting on the line, sang the loudest.
4 How on earth can I handle all that?
5 "Are we going to school?" she asked.
6 William said, "It's just as well."
7 You take the shortest; we'll take the longest.
8 "It's about time too," I replied.
9 "Those were the days," she said, with a sigh.
10 And that's all for now, I'm afraid. or And that's all. For now I'm afraid.

MATHS

UNIT 1

1	300	70	8
2	800	70	3
3	300	80	7
4	700	30	8
5	700	80	3
6	800	30	7

378   387   738   783   837   873

7 199, 254, 382, 503
8 242, 244, 424, 442
9 99, 101, 309, 321
10 63, 306, 360, 603
11 527, 627, 727
12 388, 398, 408
13 809, 909, 1009
14 590, 591, 592
15 316, 326, 336
16 118, 128, 138

UNIT 2

1 2, 4, 6, 8, 10, 12, 14, 16, 18, 20, 22
2 4, 8, 12, 16, 20, 24, 28, 32, 36, 40, 44
3 10, 20, 30, 40, 50, 60, 70, 80, 90, 100, 110
4 8, 16, 24, 32, 40, 48, 56, 64, 72, 80, 88
5 50, 100, 150, 200, 250, 300, 350, 400, 450, 500
6 100, 200, 300, 400, 500, 600, 700, 800, 900
7 15, 24, 30, 36
8 10, 25, 30, 40, 55
9 150, 200, 350, 500
10 24, 48, 64, 80

UNIT 3

1	11	14	13
	14	17	16
	10	13	12
	12	15	14
	13	16	15
	5	7	3
	3	5	1
	4	6	2
	6	8	4
	2	4	0

2	22	18	21
	27	23	26
	20	16	19
	33	29	32
	44	40	43
	12	16	13
	5	9	6
	8	12	9
	14	18	15
	11	15	12

3

32	38	35
26	32	29
39	45	42
50	56	53
29	35	32
38	33	30
25	20	17
14	9	6
10	5	2
21	16	13

UNIT 4

1	392	16	234
2	183	17	207
3	494	18	893
4	648	19	772
5	913	20	723
6	925	21	1089
7	254	22	698
8	407	23	1172
9	895	24	842
10	681	25	611
11	368	26	901
12	799	27	463
13	282	28	195
14	163	29	858
15	492	30	409

UNIT 5

1	678	7	1024
2	975	8	813
3	908	9	1122
4	493	10	821
5	843	11	1004
6	720	12	1100

UNIT 6

1	636	8	479
2	616	9	189
3	719	10	315
4	414	11	349
5	271	12	365
6	404		
7	229		

UNIT 7

1. £33
2. £11
3. £65
4. £35
5. £9.60
6. £2.51
7. £3.85
8. £10.35
9. Dartboard and pair of shorts

UNIT 8

1

2	3	4	5	10
4	6	8	10	20
6	9	12	15	30
8	12	16	20	40
10	15	20	25	50
12	18	24	30	60
14	21	28	35	70
16	24	32	40	80
18	27	36	45	90
20	30	40	50	100
22	33	44	55	110
24	36	48	60	120

2

5	9	24
30	48	45
16	22	120
15	35	0
20	32	24
32	36	36
16	10	0
27	25	18
30	60	3
33	28	12
45	21	0

UNIT 9

1	42	7	310
2	60	8	£42
3	92	9	136 mm
4	155		
5	135		
6	136		

UNIT 10

1 $\frac{1}{8}$ 6 $\frac{1}{10}$

2 $\frac{1}{6}$ 7 $\frac{1}{3}$

3 $\frac{1}{4}$ 8 $\frac{1}{6}$

4 $\frac{1}{10}$ 9 $\frac{1}{2}$

5 $\frac{1}{5}$

10 $\frac{1}{10}$ $\frac{1}{8}$ $\frac{1}{6}$ $\frac{1}{5}$ $\frac{1}{4}$ $\frac{1}{3}$ $\frac{1}{2}$

UNIT 11

1 $\frac{2}{5}$ $\frac{5}{6}$ $\frac{3}{10}$

$\frac{5}{7}$ $\frac{6}{12}$ or $\frac{1}{2}$ 1 or $\frac{1}{1}$

2 $\frac{2}{2}$ $\frac{4}{4}$ $\frac{3}{3}$ $\frac{8}{8}$ $\frac{7}{7}$

3 3
4 3
5 1
6 7

UNIT 12

1 $\frac{3}{10}$ 6 9

2 $\frac{7}{10}$ 7 12

3 $\frac{5}{10}$ or $\frac{1}{2}$ 8 3

4 $\frac{9}{10}$ 9 25

5 5

10 $\frac{4}{10}$ $\frac{7}{10}$ $\frac{9}{10}$ $\frac{10}{10}$

11 $\frac{10}{10}$ $\frac{7}{10}$ $\frac{5}{10}$ $\frac{4}{10}$ $\frac{3}{10}$ $\frac{2}{10}$

12 True

UNIT 13

1 Square
2 Circle
3 Hexagon
4 Octagon
5 Semi-circle
6 Triangle
7 Pentagon
8 Nonagon
9 1   3   4   6   7   8
10 1   8
12 1✓ 2✓ 3✓ 4✓ 5✓ 6✓ 7✓ 8✗

UNIT 14

1 Cube
2 Cylinder
3 Cone
4 Cuboid
5 Sphere
6 Triangular prism
7 Square-based pyramid
8 Hexagonal prism
9 1   4   6   7   8
10 5
11 9
12 1
13 6   8   12
     5   6   9
     6   8   12
     5   5   8

UNIT 15

1 a   e   g
3 obtuse   acute   acute
   acute   acute   obtuse

UNIT 16

1 litres   7 g
2 mm   8 ml
3 cm   9 12 cm and
4 kg   5 cm
5 cm   10 34 cm
6 litres   11 24 cm

UNIT 17

1 Twenty to four
2 Five past six
3 Five to twelve

4 Nine minutes past three

5

6

7

8

9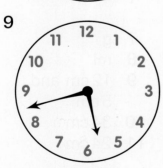

10 7:30   7:50   3:15   1:25   5:43

UNIT 18

1	31	**13**	61
2	30	**14**	61
3	31	**15**	62
4	31	**16**	62
5	30	**17**	60
6	31	**18**	92
7	30	**19**	70 days
8	31	**20**	3 months
9	30	**21**	90 seconds
10	31	**22**	2 minutes
11	31	**23**	5 minutes
12	28 or 29		

UNIT 19

1	40	**4**	45
2	80	**5**	40
3	30	**6**	15

7

Number of DVDs sold on Saturday:
- horror: 40
- drama: 80
- children's: 30
- comedy: 45

8 Own questions

HOW HAVE I DONE?

1 400 30 6

2 189, 263, 265, 273

3 709, 809, 909,

4 8, 16, 24, 32, 40, 48, 56, 64, 72, 80, 88, 96

5

+	8	4	7
6	14	10	13
9	17	13	16
17	25	21	24

−	7	8	5
10	3	2	5
13	6	5	8
24	17	16	19

6 486, 472, 186, 403

7 777, 548
763, 656

8 24, 60, 80, 75, 92

9 $\frac{1}{5}$, $\frac{2}{3}$

10 $\frac{2}{10}$ (or 1/5), $\frac{4}{10}$ (or 2/5),

$\frac{6}{10}$ (or 2/5), $\frac{7}{10}$, $\frac{9}{10}$

11 centimetres (or cm), metres (or m)

12

13 61

PROBLEM SOLVING

UNIT 1
1 300
2 100
3 587
4 71
5 900
6 1500 km
7 Fifty-eight thousand four hundred and thirty-six
8 Nine hundred and seventy-five
9 3679

UNIT 2
1 4
2 $\frac{4}{5}$
3 3
4 25
5 500 m
6 6
7 $\frac{1}{5}$
8 5
9 Kim, by 6 minutes

UNIT 3
1 £13.70
2 65 cm
3 14.4 m
4 25p
5 7.5 m
6 13.5 m
7 6.8 l
8 3.4 kg
9 £232.80

UNIT 4
1 16
2 45
3 81
4 43
5 121
6 27
7 402
8 851
9 17

Have a go: Example:
a) 12 + 10 − 2 = 20
b) 75 − 20 + 45 = 100

UNIT 5
1 £1.80
2 9
3 £1.50
4 £4.36
5 £7
6 £11.50
7 A car and a boat for £4.74. She would get 26p change.
8 £11.94
9 £45.13

UNIT 6
1 45 minutes
2 75 minutes
3 12.00 p.m.
4 1.05 p.m.
5 2.35 p.m.
6 4.50 p.m.
7 11.15 a.m.
8 12.25 p.m.
9 30 August

UNIT 7
1   35 cm
2   1.6 m
3   105 m
4   106.5 m
5   120 mm (12 cm)
6   2.72 m
7   60 cm
8   20 m × 2 and 15.5 m
9   876 m

UNIT 8
1   92 g
2   550 g
3   2.1 kg
4   3.1 kg
5   78.908 kg
6   85
7   553 kg
8   560
9   498 kg

UNIT 9
1   1 litre
2   65 l
3   3.2 l
4   1.2 l
5   54.9 l
6   1.85 l
7   35 l
8   12
9   2.5 l lemonade, 350 ml fruit juice, 125 ml lemon juice

UNIT 10
1   26
2   12
3   36
4   7
5   64
6   63
7   12, 24, 36 and 48
8   24 and 12
9   76 × 15 ÷ 20 = 57

UNIT 11
1   11, 8, 5. The numbers decrease by three each time.
2   49, 56, 63. Seventy-seven.
3   3, 8, 13, 18, 23, 28, 33. The numbers increase by five each time.
4   7, 18, 29, 40, 51, 62. The numbers increase by eleven each time.
5   18, 11, 4
6   221, 209, 197
7   −2, −4, −6
8   4001, 5001, 6001
9   64, 81, 100 (Square numbers)
Have a go: M (May), J (June)

UNIT 12
1   24
2   27
3   8
4   4
5   60p
6   16
7   £144
8   7 sets with 2 left over
9   Day 10, day 20, day 30, day 40

UNIT 13
1   a) 4 b) 2
2   A circle

4   Example:

5   Example: 2 × triangle (6) + 2 × square (8) = 14 sides
6   Example: Answer 1: triangles. Answer 2: a square which was cut diagonally to form two isosceles triangles.
7   Example:

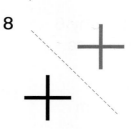

8

9   30

UNIT 14
1   14
2   Pentagonal prism and a cone

3 Two examples: cube, sphere and triangular-based pyramid; pentagonal prism, cuboid and cone

4 Square-based pyramid

5

NAME	NUMBER OF FACES	SHAPE OF FACES	NUMBER OF EDGES	NUMBER OF VERTICES
Triangular prism	5	triangular and rectangular	9	6
Square-based pyramid	5	square and triangles	8	5
Cube	6	square	12	8
Cuboid	6	square and rectangular	12	8
Hexagonal prism	8	hexagonal and rectangular	18	12

6 Example: square-based pyramid and cube

7 Cuboid and cube

8 A cone

9 Example:

UNIT 15

1 South
2 South
3 North
4 North-west
5 2 squares south to C
6 5 squares east to D
7 5 squares south-west over hilly ground
8 a) They see a farmhouse on their right and travel 5 squares north-west.
b) They cross the river at the bridge.
9 4 squares north-east across the bridge, 4 squares east and then 5 squares south to the finish.

UNIT 16

1 An apple
2 2
3 27

4 The least favourite snack was sunflower seeds.
5 Between 10.45 a.m. and 11.00 a.m.
6 45
7 55
8 8.45 to 9.00 a.m. and 3.30 to 3.45 p.m.
9 165

Have a go: Two suggestions could be: Change sunflower seeds snack for more fruit and because of the amount of heavy traffic before and after school, petition the council to build a footbridge for safe road crossing.

UNIT 17

1 25
2 61
3 103
4 £1.95
5 3
6 One packet of 8 for £1.29
7 £7
8 $\frac{5}{6}$
9 12

HOW HAVE I DONE?

1 984
2 $\frac{4}{5}$
3 £11.80
4 18
5 £3.07
6 1 hour 35 minutes
7 3.11 m
8 3.7 kg
9 15.4 l
10 7
11 38 and 64
12 3
13 Pentagons
14 6
15 South-east
16 35
17 The mints cost 15p more.
18 Tricky! You have to make a 3D shape.

Notes